RI
BALTICS & RUSSIA

1997

Rick Steves and Ian Watson

John Muir Publications
Santa Fe, New Mexico

Other JMP travel guidebooks by Rick Steves
Asia Through the Back Door (with Bob Effertz)
Europe Through the Back Door
Europe 101: History and Art for the Traveler
    (with Gene Openshaw)
Mona Winks: Self-Guided Tours of Europe's Top Museums
    (with Gene Openshaw)
Rick Steves' Europe
Rick Steves' France, Belgium & the Netherlands (with Steve Smith)
Rick Steves' Germany, Austria & Switzerland
Rick Steves' Great Britain & Ireland
Rick Steves' Italy
Rick Steves' Scandinavia
Rick Steves' Spain & Portugal
Rick Steves' Phrase Books for: French, German, Italian,
    Spanish/Portuguese, and French/German/Italian

Thanks to my hardworking team at Europe Through the Back Door; the
many readers who shared tips and experiences from their travels; the many
Europeans who make travel such a good living; and most of all, to my wife,
Anne, for her support.

Special thanks: Adam Tolnay, Pernille Knutsson, Steven Caron, Zachary
Haberer, Katrin Kaarli, Peetri Ruohonen, Matthias Lüfkens.

John Muir Publications, P.O. Box 613, Santa Fe, NM 87504
Copyright © 1997, 1996, 1994 by Rick Steves and Ian Watson
Maps © 1994 Rick Steves' Europe Through the Back Door, Inc.
Cover © 1997 by John Muir Publications
All rights reserved.

Printed in the United States of America
First printing February 1997

ISSN 1085-7230
ISBN 1-56261-325-1

For the latest on Rick's lectures, guidebooks, tours, and PBS-TV series,
contact Europe Through the Back Door, Box 2009, Edmonds, WA 98020,
tel. 206/771-8303, fax 206/771-0833, online at ricksteves@aol.com or on the
web at http://www.ricksteves.com.

Europe Through the Back Door Editors Risa Laib, Rich Sorensen, Rick
Steves
John Muir Publications Editors Chris Hayhurst, Dianna Delling
Production Marie J. T. Vigil, Nikki Rooker
Maps Dave C. Hoerlein
Cover Design Cowgirls Design, Kathryn Lloyd-Strongin
Design Linda Braun
Typesetting Marilyn Hagger, Marie J.T. Vigil
Printer Banta Company
Cover Photo Red Square, Moscow; Unicorn/Jeff Greenberg

Distributed to the book trade by
Publishers Group West
Emeryville, California

CONTENTS

Introduction 1

*Planning Your Trip 3 • Trip Costs 3 • Prices, Times, and
Discounts 5 • When to Go 5 • Sightseeing Priorities 5 •
Red Tape and Business Hours 6 • Banking 7 • Language
7 • Travel Smart 8 • Pack Along 8 • Tourist Information
9 • Recommended Guidebooks 9 • Rick Steves' Books
and Videos 10 • Maps 11 • Info Off the Internet 11 •
Transportation 11 • Border Controls 15 • Telephones
and Mail 15 •Sleeping 17 • Eating 18 • Safety and
Health 20 • Surviving Russia 21 • Stranger in a Strange
Land 23 • Back Door Manners 23 • Send Us a Postcard,
Drop Us a Line 23 • Back Door Travel Philosophy 25*

Getting Your Visa 26

Gateways to the Baltics and Russia:
    Helsinki, Stockholm, and Warsaw 33

Russia 49

    Moscow 50

    St. Petersburg 69

Baltics 91

    Tallinn, Estonia 92

    Riga, Latvia 107

    Vilnius, Lithuania 119

Trans-Siberian Railway 132

Appendix 137

*Baltic Timeline 137 • Russian Timeline 138 • Let's Talk
Telephones 140 • Climate 142 • Metric Conversions 143
• Numbers and Stumblers 143 • Public Holidays 143 •
Learning Cyrillic 144 • Survival Phrases 145 • Buying
Train Tickets 146 • Road Scholar Feedback Form 147 •
Faxing Your Hotel Reservation 149*

Index 150

Europe

500 KM
300 MI

ARCTIC CIRCLE

LAPLAND

Trondheim

NORWAY
BOGNA FJORD

Bergen
Oslo

FINLAND

Helsinki

Turku

St. Petersburg

Stockholm

SWEDEN

Tallinn

ESTONIA

RUSSIA

BALTIC

SEA

Riga

LATVIA

Moscow

SCOTLAND

Edinburgh

DENMARK

Copenhagen

LITHUANIA

Vilnius

IRE.

NORTH

RUSS.

IRELAND

Dublin

York

SEA

DINGLE PENINSULA

WALES

ENGLAND

Lübeck

POLAND

BELARUS

London

Amsterdam

Berlin

Warsaw

Bath

Bruges

NETH.

GERMANY

Brussels

Krakow

UKRAINE

Kiev

BELG.

RHINE

Prague

Mont St. Michel

NORMANDY

LUX.

MOSEL

CZECH.

SLOVAK.

MOLDOVA

Paris

ALSACE

ROM.
ROAD

ATLANTIC

BRITTANY

Colmar

Munich

Vienna

Budapest

BAVARIA

LOIRE

Salzburg

HUNG.

ROMANIA

BLACK

OCEAN

FRANCE

Bern

BERN
OBER.

TIROL

AUST.

SWITZ.

DOLO-
MITES

SLOV.

CRO.

Belgrade

Bucharest

Chamonix

Milan

SEA

DORDOGNE

Venice

BOSNIA
HERZ.

PROVENCE

CINQUE
TERRE

Florence

SERBIA

Sofia

Carc.

Arles

SAN
MARINO

Dubrovnik

BULG.

MONACO

UMBRIA

ADRIATIC

Istanbul

ANDORRA

Nice

CORSICA

Rome

ITALY

ALB.

CAPPA-
DOCIA

SPAIN

Madrid

Barcelona

Naples

GREECE

AEGEAN

TURKEY

PORTUGAL

Toledo

SARDINIA

AMALF
COAST

CORFU

Athens

Ephesus

Lisbon

PEL.

SEA

Seville

Gran.

MEDITERRANEAN

SICILY

ALGARVE

ANDALUSIA

CRETE

MOROCCO

ALGERIA

TUNISIA

SEA

INTRODUCTION

This book breaks the Baltics and Russia into its top destinations. We focus only on the three Baltic capital cities and Russia's two most important stops. For the average first visit, these five cities are the predictable and best targets. This book will give you all the information and opinions necessary to wring the maximum value out of your limited time and money in each of these destinations. If you plan two weeks or less for the Baltics and Russia, and have a normal appetite for information, this lean and mean little book is all you need. If you're a travel info fiend, this book sorts through all the superlatives and provides a handy rack upon which to hang your supplemental information.

We wrote this book to fill several needs. There is very little written on independent budget travel in the Baltics and Russia, and much of what is available on this quickly developing region is out of date by the time it hits the bookshelf. The Baltics and Russia offer a world of travel thrills with plenty of hardworking local people eager to develop their entrepreneurial skills. They have a long way to go, and they could certainly use a few customers (with Western cash) to practice on. We hope this book will help give the local economies a much-needed boost by giving American travelers confidence, through fresh and clear information, to travel to the Baltics and Russia. We know the area is a great travel destination. And it will never be more interesting than in 1997.

American newspapers sometimes give an over-gloomy impression of life in Russia and the Baltic states, focusing on crime, unemployment, fuel shortages, foul-temperedness, and ominous political events. In reality, for most locals, life goes on: people buy bread, go to work a bit, ride the subway, get married, dabble in business speculation, visit their grandmothers, and grumble as much about the hardships of life now as they did about the "system" under Communism. Meanwhile, life gets better and better for tourists. Getting a visa, getting there, getting around, finding a place to stay, eating out, and meeting the locals are all markedly easier than they were even a year ago. We're not trying to convince you that the Baltics and Russia are the kind of places you should choose first for your hard-earned two-week vacation. But people who've made up their minds already, who have chosen to go and have a reason to visit—friends, relatives, business, research, study, or just curiosity—can have a great time, and this book is here to help.

Since the Baltics declared independence from the Soviet Union in 1991, travel in the Baltics has gotten more and more like travel in the rest of Europe. You don't need a visa. Well-kept restaurants and hotels offer value for your money. Just buy your plane ticket, reserve a place to stay for your first night, and go. In Russia, because of outdated visa restrictions (more about this later), moderately-priced hotels that accept reservations in a simple and straightforward way have not developed as fast as we hoped. Planning a trip to Russia isn't *that* hard, but it's a lot different than planning a trip to Italy, and you have much less flexibility about where you can stay. So our coverage of Russia is geared to two types of people. For independent budget travelers who like the idea of staying in the Moscow Travellers Guest House or the St. Petersburg International Hostel, we show you how these safe, well-run places help you organize your trip around the two crucial practicalities: an inexpensive but respectable place to stay, and convenient visa support. For those of you who already have visa support and accommodations in Russia set up (through friends, a travel agent, a package tour, or a study group), and don't need our help with accommodations, this book is useful as a concise guide to eating, sightseeing, and getting around St. Petersburg and Moscow.

This Information Is Accurate and Up-to-Date

This book is updated every year. Most publishers of guidebooks that cover a region from top to bottom can afford an update only every two or three years (and even then, it's often by letter). Since this book is selective, covering only the places we think make up the top two weeks, we're able to update it each summer. Even with an annual update, things change. But if you're traveling with the current edition of this book, we guarantee you're using the most up-to-date information available. This book will help you have an inexpensive, hassle-free trip. *Use this year's edition.* We tell you, you're crazy to save a few bucks by traveling on old information. If you're packing an old book, you'll learn the seriousness of your mistake . . . on the first day of your trip. Your trip costs about $10 per waking hour. Your time is valuable. This guidebook saves lots of time.

Planning Your Trip

This book is organized by destinations. Each of these destinations is a mini-vacation on its own, filled with exciting sights and affordable places to stay. In each chapter, you'll find:

Planning Your Time, a suggested schedule with thoughts on how to best use your limited time.

Orientation, including tourist information, city transportation, and an easy-to-read map designed to make the text clear and your arrival smooth.

Sights with ratings: ▲▲▲—Don't miss; ▲▲—Try hard to see; ▲—Worthwhile if you can make it; No rating—Worth knowing about.

Sleeping and **Eating** with addresses and phone numbers of our favorite budget hotels and restaurants.

And **Transportation Connections** to nearby destinations by train and bus.

The handy Appendix is a traveler's tool kit, with historic timelines, telephone tips, a climate chart, and survival phrases.

Browse through this book, choose your favorite destinations, and link them up. Then have a great trip! You'll travel like a temporary local, getting the absolute most out of every mile, minute, and dollar. You won't waste time on mediocre sights because, unlike other guidebooks, we cover only the best. Since lousy, expensive hotels are a major financial pitfall, we've worked hard to assemble the best accommodations values for each stop. And, as you travel the route we know and love, we're happy you'll be meeting some of our favorite people.

Trip Costs

Five components make up your trip costs: airfare, surface transportation, room and board, sightseeing, and shopping/entertainment/miscellany.

Airfare: Don't try to sort through the mess. Find and use a good travel agent. A basic round-trip from the U.S.A. to Moscow or St. Petersburg costs around $1,100, depending on where you fly from and when. Always consider saving time and money by flying open-jaws (into one city and out of another). Or fly into a cheaper European port and add the Baltics and Russia to a longer European trip. (See Itinerary Tips, below.)

Surface Transportation: For a two-week whirlwind trip of our recommended destinations, allow $200 per person for public transportation (trains and key buses).

Room and Board: You can thrive in the Baltics and Russia on $60 a day per person for room and board. A $60-a-day budget allows an average of $10 for lunch, $15 for dinner, and $35 for lodging (based on two people splitting the cost of a $70 double room that includes breakfast). Consider $70 for a double room a rough average—you could pay $15 per person for a hostel one night and $100 for a hotel room the next night. Students and tightwads travel on $40 a day ($15 to $20 per bed, $20 a day for meals and snacks). But budget sleeping and eating require the skills and information covered later in this chapter.

Sightseeing: In big cities, figure $5 to $10 per major sight (such as St. Petersburg's Hermitage), $2 for minor ones (climbing church towers), $10 for guided walks, and $20 for splurge experiences like the ballet. An overall average of $15 a day works for most. Don't skimp here. After all, this category directly powers most of the experiences all the other expenses are designed to make possible.

Shopping/Entertainment/Miscellany: This can vary from nearly nothing to a small fortune. Figure $1 per postcard, $1 per ice cream cone, $2 per coffee and soft drink, and $10 to $30 for evening entertainment.

Exchange Rates

We've priced many things throughout this book in the local currency.

One U.S. dollar = approximately . . .

12 Estonian kroons (kr)	4 Lithuanian litas (Lt)
4.5 Finnish marks (mk)	5,000 Russian rubles
0.55 Latvian lats (Ls)	6.5 Swedish kronor (kr)

Estonia, Latvia, and Lithuania have fairly stable, permanent currencies. In Russia, the ruble's value varies considerably, so many prices are listed in Russia in dollars and then converted into rubles at that day's exchange rate. In this book, too, all Russian prices are listed in dollars, but you will always pay in rubles. Although dollars do circulate as an unofficial currency in Russia, you should politely refuse if taxi drivers or kiosk owners ask you to pay in dollars.

Prices, Times, and Discounts

The prices in this book, as well as the hours and telephone numbers, are accurate as of mid-1996. The Baltics and Russia are changing rapidly, and we know you'll understand that this, like any other guidebook, starts to yellow even before it's printed.

In the Baltics and Russia, you'll be using the 24-hour clock. After 12:00 noon, keep going—13:00, 14:00. . . . For anything over 12, subtract 12 and add p.m. (14:00 is 2:00 p.m.)

This book lists peak-season hours for sightseeing attractions (July and August). Off-season, roughly October through April, expect shorter hours, more lunchtime breaks, and fewer activities. Confirm your sightseeing plans locally, especially when traveling between October and April.

Students with International Student Identification Cards (ISIC) often get big discounts on sights—but only by asking.

In Russia the old Communist dual pricing system is still in effect for trains, hotels, some theater tickets, and sightseeing. For example, in 1996 admission to the Hermitage in St. Petersburg normally cost 10,000 rubles or $2, which was consistent with the rest of the Russian economy's price level. However, foreigners were charged 40,000 rubles or about $8. The ethical and economic soundness of this policy is debatable. Regardless, it's almost impossible to sneak through at the regular price; if your clothes or your accent don't give you away, your passport certainly will. Although prices in Estonia, Latvia, and Lithuania are also low relative to the West, foreigner markups have almost disappeared from the Baltics since 1991.

When to Go

Summers are cool in the Baltics and Russia. Some days will be warm enough to wear just a T-shirt, but definitely pack a sweater for the evenings. Moscow summers bring thunderstorms like clockwork late in the afternoon. Don't trust the blue sky when you wake up; bring that umbrella. Winters are dark, cold, and dreary, and in Russia you'll still be dodging puddles of melting ice on the sidewalk as late as April. In spring and fall, too, you'll need to bundle up. See the climate chart in the Appendix for more information.

Sightseeing Priorities

Depending on the length of your trip, here are our recommended priorities.

4 days:	Tallinn and St. Petersburg
7 days, add:	Vilnius
9 days, add:	Riga
14 days, add:	Moscow, and slow down

Itinerary Tips

You can approach Russia and the Baltics from Scandinavia, Central Europe, or even China. Helsinki is the best jumping-off point: you can get to Tallinn by hydrofoil in two hours, and to St. Petersburg by rail in less than seven hours. From Warsaw you can take a ten-hour bus ride to Vilnius or a 19-hour train ride to Moscow. From Stockholm you can ride the overnight ferry to Tallinn. It may help to think of your trip as an excursion from Helsinki or Warsaw, or as an interesting way to connect Europe and Scandinavia. The Gateways chapter of this book has information on these routes.

Those doing Europe with a railpass can plan an "open-jaws" trip, using the pass in Western Europe first, finishing off with a Baltics swing, and flying home from any of the cities featured in this book.

Two weeks is plenty of time to visit the five cities covered in this book. Moscow, St. Petersburg, and Tallinn are worth three days each; Riga and Vilnius can be seen in two. This region lends itself well to overnight train rides. Whenever possible, connect towns as you sleep.

Figure out where you'll start and where you'll finish. If you're visiting only Russia, it's better to go from Helsinki than from Warsaw. If you're visiting only the Baltics, either will do. Of course, you can also fly from the U.S.A. into or out of any of the cities in this book (usually with one connection).

Whatever you do, plan to make just one pass through Russia, so that you will have to get only one Russian visa. And if you have a choice, visit St. Petersburg before you go to Moscow. It's smaller, prettier, and can give you an idea whether you like Russia and really want to take the plunge and go to Moscow. Also, going from Russia to the Baltics, rather than from the Baltics to Russia, will allow you to share in the sense of liberation that Estonians, Latvians, and Lithuanians felt in 1991.

Red Tape and Business Hours

Americans need visas to travel in Russia. For more information, see the Getting Your Visa chapter.

It's common for Russian shops to open on Sundays—the legacy of atheism. In the Baltics, fewer stores are open on Sundays. Especially in Russia and at state-run shops, there is an hour-long break for lunch, either 13:00–14:00 or 14:00–15:00.

At many stores in Russia and at some in the Baltics you must stand in three lines: first, at the counter, to decide what you want and total up the price; second, to pay the cashier and get a slip; and third, to present the slip at the counter and get the goods. If you're buying food, you have to go through this once at the meat counter, once at the cheese counter, and so on. The Western system of selecting your own goods from the shelf and paying for them at one central location is catching on slowly. Supermarkets are a recent, welcome innovation.

Banking

It's possible to change money at currency exchange desks in Russia and the Baltics at almost any time of day. You should avoid changing at "mini-market"-type kiosks or with wad-wavers on the street.

Exchange rates are usually pretty similar from bank to bank. In this part of the world the sign of a good deal on exchange is no commission and no more than a 1 to 1.5 percent spread between buying and selling rates. Over 2.5 to 3 percent starts to smack of tourist rip-off.

It's now possible to exchange American Express traveler's checks in all five cities covered in this book. In Tallinn, most banks will accept traveler's checks with a minimal commission (e.g., 1 percent). In Riga, Vilnius, St. Petersburg, and particularly Moscow, fewer banks take traveler's checks, and commissions are stiffer. If you bring traveler's checks at all, don't bring more than half your money in them. U.S. cash dollars are better, and you can carry them safely in a neck pouch or money belt (call us at 206/771-8303 for a free catalog/newsletter). Bring only new or nearly new currency. Worn, inky, heavily creased, or pre-1990 dollars are frequently not accepted in Russia. Carry smaller bills—a few twenties, tens, fives, and ones—since people who deal with hard currency often don't have exact change.

Language Barrier

Many young people in the Baltics and Russia have studied English and can communicate basic phrases. Particularly in

Estonia, most young people speak enough to deal with basic questions, and in the Baltics in general anyone in the tourist trade will probably know some English. In Estonia and Latvia, many people over 60 speak some German. Just about everyone in the Baltic states speaks Russian. Sensationalists warn that Balts will practically spit in your face if you speak Russian to them. This is only true of a tiny minority of militant nationalists. Try English first, but if you speak Russian, use it.

Latvian and Lithuanian are Baltic languages. Like Spanish and Italian, they are similar but not mutually intelligible. Russian is a Slavic language. The Slavic languages, the Baltic languages, and English all descend from Indo-European. Estonian, on the other hand, is a Finno-Ugric language, completely unrelated to the others (but a lot like Finnish with the last letter of every word cut off). Look at the Estonian words for one, two, and three in the Appendix word list; the similarities and differences jump right out.

Check the Appendix for survival phrases. We've also included the Cyrillic alphabet and some pronunciation tips. Those who make a point to memorize these things will travel more smoothly.

Travel Smart

Upon arrival in a new town, lay the groundwork for a smooth departure. Reread this book as you travel, and take advantage of local tourist information sources. Buy a phone card and use it for reservations and confirmations. Enjoy the friendliness of the local people. Ask questions. Most locals are eager to point you in their idea of the right direction. Wear your money belt, pack a pocket-size notepad to organize your thoughts, and practice the virtue of simplicity. Those who expect to travel smart, do. Plan ahead for banking, laundry, post office chores, and picnics. To maximize rootedness, minimize one-night stands. Mix intense and relaxed periods. Every trip (and every traveler) needs at least a few slack days. Pace yourself. Assume you will return.

Pack Along

Except for a few exceptions, pack for a trip to the Baltics and Russia as you would for a trip through Western Europe.

For Yourself: Consider bringing an emergency roll of toilet paper, vitamins, and plastic bags (though you can get them on the spot, too) or a net bag.

For Gifts: These days you can get anything in the hard-currency stores, so the best sure-fire pleaser is Western cash. Top quality, duty-free candy and chocolate, always easy to get on the ferry from Scandinavia, are much appreciated. Postcards, stickers, pins, T-shirts, hats, and decals from the U.S.A. (the more Western-looking the better), well-chosen perfume or makeup, coffee, seeds (both vegetable and flower), tapes, and Western-printed Russian-English dictionaries are also good gifts.

Tourist Information
The tourist information office is your best first stop in any new city. You'll find city-funded tourist offices in Tallinn and Riga. In Moscow, St. Petersburg, and Vilnius you're on your own, though in St. Petersburg a private tourist office called Peter T.i.P.S. has bravely taken on the job of giving free advice to individual tourists.

Recommended Guidebooks
You may want some supplemental travel guidebooks, especially if you're traveling beyond our recommended destinations. When you consider the improvements they'll make in your $3,000 vacation, $25 or $35 for extra maps and books is money well spent. One simple budget tip can easily save the price of an extra guidebook.

Let's Go: Eastern Europe 1997 is written by students, geared for young backpackers, and covers 17 countries, including the Baltics and western Russia. Your *Rick Steves' Baltics & Russia* co-author Ian Watson is a former editor of *Let's Go: Europe.*

Lonely Planet's *Russia, Ukraine, and Belarus* (1996) and *Baltic States and Kaliningrad* (look for the 1997 edition) are good sources if you want more information on these regions, especially outside of the capital cities. *The Insight Guide: Baltic States* has informative essays and good photographs, but it's too heavy to carry.

Local English-language newspapers such as the weekly *Baltic Times*, the almost-daily *Moscow Times*, and the twice-weekly *St. Petersburg Times* are a great source for the latest news, and also carry entertainment schedules.

The Baltic Revolution (1993), by journalist Anatol Lieven, is still a good book on modern Baltic history, politics, and

society. For Russia, no one recent commentary or history
stands out as really worth buying. Instead, read one of the
shorter, more digestible Russian classics, such as Turgenev's
Fathers and Sons or Goncharov's *Oblomov*; Chekhov's plays or
short stories; or even Nabokov's autobiography, *Speak,
Memory*.

Rick Steves' Books and Videos

Rick Steves' Europe Through the Back Door 1997 (John Muir
Publications) gives you budget travel tips on minimizing jet
lag, packing light, planning your itinerary, traveling by car or
train, finding budget beds without reservations, changing
money, avoiding rip-offs, outsmarting thieves, hurdling the
language barrier, taking great photographs, staying healthy,
using bidets, and lots more. The book also includes chapters
on 40 of Rick's favorite "Back Doors."

Rick Steves' Country Guides are a series of eight
guidebooks covering Great Britain and Ireland; France, Belgium, and the Netherlands; Italy; Spain and Portugal; Germany, Austria, and Switzerland; Scandinavia; and Europe,
just as this one covers the Baltics and Russia. These are
updated annually and come out each January. If you plan to
use Scandinavia as a gateway to the Baltics and Russia, *Rick
Steves' Scandinavia 1997* (John Muir Publications) is the
guidebook for you.

Europe 101: History and Art for the Traveler (co-written
with Gene Openshaw, John Muir Publications, 1996) gives
you the story of Europe's people, history, and art. Written
for smart people who were sleeping in their history and art
classes before they knew they were going to Europe, *101*
really helps Europe's sights come alive.

Mona Winks (also co-written with Gene Openshaw, John
Muir Publications, 1996) gives you fun, easy-to-follow self-
guided tours of Europe's top 20 museums (in London, Paris,
Madrid, Amsterdam, Venice, Florence, and Rome).

Rick's slideshow lecture, "Scandinavia, Baltics, & Russia"
is available as a two-hour videotape (call us at 206/771-8303
for our free newsletter/catalog). Rick's television series,
Travels in Europe with Rick Steves, covers Europe's highlights.
His 39-show series may re-air on your local PBS station, and
the shows are also available as information-packed videotapes
(listed in our catalog).

Maps

The maps in this book, drawn by Dave Hoerlein, are concise and simple. Dave has designed the maps to help you locate recommended sights and places to stay. As you travel, you'll be able to find more in-depth maps at local tourist information offices or newsstands.

Maps of the Baltic capitals are easy to get in the Baltics. However, it's worth picking up maps of Moscow and St. Petersburg in the West (try to get a recent map with street names in both Cyrillic and Roman) since these can be hard to find in Russia.

Info Off the Internet

You can now get a lot of Baltics and Russia travel information off the Web. A great St. Petersburg site is at http://www.spb.su, with links to *The St. Petersburg Press*, the city's youth hostels, and more. For Russia, try starting at http://www.friends-partners.org/friends. Abridged online copies of *In Your Pocket* guides to Vilnius, Kaunas, and Riga (plus instructions for ordering the real things) are at http://www.omnitel.net/OurSite/Travel/viyp. There's an excellent guide to Estonia (including a calendar of events and transportation timetables) at http://www.ciesin.ee/ESTCG/. At http://www.vernet.lv/latvia/travel there's a good general guide to touring Latvia. And the Finnish train schedules (including Russian connections) are at http://www.hut.fi/Misc/VR/taulut. html. These links were current as of summer 1996.

Transportation

By Train

Overnight trains are a Russian institution. You'll board sometime in the evening, perhaps after an early dinner. Bring a late-night snack, a banana for breakfast, and enough to drink. Car doors open 20 to 30 minutes before departure. Armed with your train number, locate your platform on the announcement board in the station and show your ticket to the conductor as you step onto your car. As soon as the train is underway, she'll return to collect your ticket (giving it back before you arrive), to demand the local equivalent of a dollar or two for your clean sheets, and (in luxury compartments) to bring you tea on request. A few hours later, the lights go out

Major Transportation Connections

From	To (or vice versa)	Mode	Hours	US$
Helsinki	Tallinn	hydrofoil	2	$25
Helsinki	St. Petersburg	day train	7	$60
St. Petersburg	Moscow	night train	8	$32
Tallinn	St. Petersburg	night train	10	$15
Tallinn	Riga	day bus	6	$8
Riga	Vilnius	day bus	6	$8
Vilnius	Warsaw	day bus	10	$14

and you can sleep—until you hit the border and the customs guards knock on your door.

Soviet sleeper compartments were, and are, among the nicest in Europe. Available only on better trains, two-bed, first-class compartments called *lyuks* or CB are an affordable luxury. Four-bed, second-class *kupe* compartments are still much roomier than Western Europe's six-bunk couchettes.

Departures from each city are listed in the respective chapter, and although new schedules come out annually at the end of May, year-to-year changes are minor. Still, be sure to confirm times at the station. Prices, on the other hand, are going up every month, so use the listed ones as approximations. Times are all local. Trains usually run on time. Note that in the former Soviet Union, express trains carry people almost exclusively from the first station to the last (in other words, almost everyone on a Moscow–St. Petersburg train gets on at Moscow and will get off in St. Petersburg).

Your biggest hassle will be buying tickets. There are usually separate windows for local, for national, and for international trains. And in Russia, there's an added complication: Foreigners can only buy train tickets at the special windows for foreigners—although the clerks there generally speak no language but Russian, and the tickets are the same as Russians get but more expensive. In each city chapter, we've described the intricacies of the local system and possible solutions. There are no student discounts for foreigners.

Note that prices and policies differ from city to city, even for the same tickets on the same train. For example, you can buy a round-trip Tallinn–Moscow–Tallinn ticket in Tallinn, but not a Moscow–Tallinn–Moscow ticket in Moscow. What's more, a Moscow–Tallinn ticket bought in Tallinn costs less than in Moscow.

Especially in Russia, keep hassles to a minimum by handing the clerk a sheet of paper (see sample in Appendix) with your destination, date of travel, preferred train number or departure time, the number of seats you want, your desired class (write a K for four-bed *kupes*, or CB for luxury two-bed compartments), and your last name. Cheaper tickets for П, O, or C classes are available on virtually any train. Especially on long journeys and overnight trains, avoid these cheaper classes unless you enjoy hard, non-reclining seats. The word for train station in Russia is *vokzal*.

When you get your ticket, you may have trouble deciphering it. We've included a sample train ticket for easy reference.

Deciphering Your Train Ticket

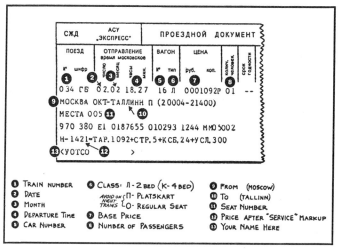

By Bus

The train system is still king in Russia, but buses have taken over in the Baltics. Faster and sometimes more comfortable, they're now the preferred way to travel between Tallinn, Riga, Vilnius, and Warsaw. In fact the Tallinn–Riga and Tallinn–Vilnius night trains have been discontinued, and even the Tallinn–Warsaw Baltic Express is running at a loss due to lack of demand, and could be phased out. Between Russia and the Baltics, train service is running at about half of its pre-independence frequency.

Buying bus tickets is generally simple and casual, and many people just show up at the station a half-hour or hour in advance, although it is prudent to reserve ahead if you are able. Make sure to find out which platform your bus leaves from (it's usually written on your ticket). Your ticket will also list a seat number but only sometimes do people sit in their assigned places. Buses range from almost-new Volvos and Mercedes, through vintage Finnish hand-me-downs to wheezing Soviet relics. For example, in 1996 our Tallinn–Vilnius bus was spotless and plush with onboard toilet, fridge, and coffee-maker and two very polite uniformed Estonian drivers, while on the Vilnius–Riga route we had a dirty Belarussian bus with a driver who smoked on board and cursed Russian passengers who couldn't speak Lithuanian.

The bus is also an option to be considered between Helsinki and St. Petersburg, especially for students, who get a big discount.

In Cities

Most cities are walkable. The only place where you absolutely have to take public transportation is Moscow. In every city you can buy single bus tickets (punch them on board) from kiosks and metro tokens from booths inside the entrances. Or, for a few dollars, you can buy a card good for unlimited public transportation for one calendar month.

Taxis: Taxis are still fairly cheap. In the Baltics, drivers at taxi stands may try to cheat you, or may work for private taxi companies with higher fares, so it is sensible to always call for a taxi. We've included the public taxi phone numbers for Tallinn, Riga, and Vilnius in their chapters. You may need help calling, since dispatchers' English is usually poor.

In Moscow and St. Petersburg, the way to get a taxi is just to stand by the side of the street with your hand out. Sometimes you will get an official driver with a meter, but more often a private citizen will pick you up, which is considered perfectly normal. When a car stops, open the door and state your destination in Russian, or at least some approximation of Russian. The driver may want to haggle; if he just says yes, though, keep silent about the fare until the end and then hand him a fair price. Don't be shy about refusing a ride if you don't trust the driver or if he asks too much money. A ride around the center of town should not cost more than the local equivalent of $2. Rides out to the suburbs shouldn't be more than $3–$5. Pay in local currency.

Airport buses: If you fly into Russia or the Baltics, remember: at *all* the airports, cheap public buses stop frequently just outside the terminal exit. In the Baltics these buses run to the center of town. In Moscow and St. Petersburg they'll drop you at an outlying metro station. Unless you're bringing barnyards of luggage, skip the airport taxi stands, where you're likely to be overcharged. (Even if you take the bus into town and then a taxi, you'll have a better chance of getting an honest deal.) You can change a little money for bus tickets in the airport terminal or with a friendly local on board.

Border Controls

Border controls between the Baltic States are quick and light, with guards hopping on board your bus to glance at your passport. Russian customs is a much more drawn-out affair with baggage declarations, searches, and an intimidating air—if you're coming by bus, you usually have to get off and line up in the customs shed. For more information, see the Getting Your Visa chapter.

Telephones and Mail

Using the telephone in the Baltics and Russia has gotten much easier. Telephone cards, which work in new digital pay phones around town, have made long-distance calls a cinch. They come in various denominations, and each country has its own cards. If you don't want to buy a phone card because you don't know how much you'll be spending on a call, head to the central post office or telephone office, where there are metered

(talk-now-pay-later) booths. Except in Riga, local calls are free
from private phones, so shops and offices will often allow you
to make a quick local call if you ask politely.

Unfortunately, with improvement in service has come a
huge increase in price. Calling between Moscow and St.
Petersburg, which used to be almost free, now runs around 50
cents per minute. One minute from Vilnius to St. Petersburg
will run you almost a dollar, and between Estonia and Lithuania calls cost about 35 cents.

The country code for Russia is 7; the city code for
Moscow is 095, for St. Petersburg 812. The Baltic states have
their own country codes. Estonia is 372, Latvia is 371, and
Lithuania is 370. Lithuania still has city codes (Vilnius' is 2),
but Estonia and Latvia are in the process of dismantling their
city code systems.

From a telephone numbering perspective, the Baltic states
still aren't independent if you're calling from Russia, from
Lithuania, or from phones in Riga that have old numbers starting with 2. From these phones you use the old Soviet area
codes (014 for Estonia, 013 for Riga, and 012 for Lithuania)
instead of 372, 371, 370. We've included a complete dialing
chart in the Appendix to help you sort things out, along with a
list of international access codes and country codes.

The numbers listed in each section of this book are always
the ones you dial when calling locally. See the special instructions in the Tallinn and Riga chapters on how to deal with the
changing numbering systems in their countries.

Calling Home Using AT&T's USA Direct Service:
AT&T offers USA Direct Service in each of the five cities in
this book. These phone numbers are listed in the Appendix. Dial
the local number (listed for the country you're calling from) to
reach an English-speaking operator who will ask for your card
number, dial your call for you, and bill your home phone number (at the rate of approximately $3 a minute plus a $2.50 service
charge). It's convenient, but it's not cheap. Hanging up when
you hear an answering machine is a $5.50 mistake—talk! Better
yet, use a Russian or Baltic phone card to call home for five seconds—long enough to say "call me," or to make sure an answering machine is off so you can call back, using your USA Direct
number to connect with a person. Finnish and Baltic time is
seven/ten hours ahead of the east/west coast of the U.S.A.;
Russian time is one more hour ahead.

Avoid using USA Direct for calls between European countries; it's much cheaper to call direct by using coins, a Russian or Baltic phone card, or a metered booth in a telephone office.

Mail: The Baltic mail systems are now up to world standards. If you need to send a box home from Russia, go to Tallinn for the weekend and send it surface mail from the main post office there. If you send a Christmas card from Russia, leave the year off.

Sleeping in the Baltics

Finding a place to stay in the Baltics resembles finding a place to stay anywhere else in Europe, although the range of choices is a little narrower and the value-for-money ratio is perhaps a little lower.

It's possible to travel at any time of year without reservations, but given the high stakes and erratic accommodations values, we'd highly recommend calling ahead for rooms a day or two in advance as you travel. We've taken great pains to list telephone numbers with long distance instructions (see Appendix). Use the convenient telephone cards. Most hotels listed are accustomed to English-only speakers.

If you know exactly which dates you need and really want a particular place, reserve a room well in advance before you leave home. To reserve from home, call, fax, or write the hotel. Phone and fax costs are reasonable, and simple English is usually fine. To fax, use the form in the Appendix.

Reconfirm your reservations a day in advance. Honor (or cancel by phone) your reservations. Long distance is cheap and easy from public phone booths. Don't let these people down—we promised you'd call and cancel if for some reason you won't show up. Don't needlessly confirm rooms through the tourist office; they'll take a commission.

Sleeping in Russia

It is really hard to recommend good places to stay in Russia. The best advice we can give is perhaps this—if you have friends in Russia, stay with them! Clean, comfortable hotels which can issue visa support for you, like the Radisson or the Aerostar in Moscow, cost much too much—like $200 a night. Affordably priced places are often disorganized, unable to help you with your visa, unprepared for individual travelers, surly, filthy, and

otherwise mired in Soviet ways. Then there are places that are
both expensive *and* repulsive. Safe, comfortable, and competently
staffed sleeping options in the range of $60–$75 for a double
room with bath have simply not developed.

Of the precious few establishments that are both reasonably cheap and reasonably well-run, the St. Petersburg International Hostel stands out for its safety, service, and efficient visa
support system. Remember, though, it's a hostel. If you don't
want to share a shower, the best way to get the combination of
a private bathroom, reasonable room rate, safety, and visa support is to buy a flight-plus-hotel package (from Finnair, for
example) and use this book simply as a sightseeing guide. Tour
operators and travel agencies are able to arrange lower prices
at better hotels more easily than you can as an independent
traveler.

Several companies have tried to start homestay and bed-
and-breakfast services in Moscow and St. Petersburg, but many
have folded after a year or two, and none have succeeded in
setting up a visa support system as effective as the hostel's. We
list two relatively reliable homestay organizations in the Getting Your Visa chapter.

Be warned that many municipal hot-water heating systems
shut down for maintenance for a few weeks each summer, and
entire towns (except for the very expensive hotels) go without
hot water.

Eating

Truly local Baltic and Russian cooking relies on bread, meat,
potatoes, berries, sour cream, and northern vegetables such as
cabbage, carrots, and beets, topped off with fruit compote, tea,
cakes, and vodka. The best way to experience an authentic
meal is on the rickety living room table in a new friend's apartment. Russians and Balts themselves almost never go out to
eat, but they love having guests for dinner. Though tasty
enough, local food is often a disaster cocktail of salt, fat, and
sour cream, which together with industrial pollution and poor
standards of exercise, sanitation, and health education, has cor-
rupted the well-being of millions of people across the former
Soviet Union.

Russian and Baltic restaurant cooking emerged from communism ravaged and mutant. Much of what was considered
best about Russian food during the Communist period actually

came from more abundant areas of the Soviet Union such as
Central Asia and the Caucasus (see our Georgian food ordering guide in the Moscow section). Amid this desolation, foreign cuisine held out the only hope of nutritional salvation.
Most of the restaurants that opened shortly after the fall of
Communism served Chinese, Italian, Indian, American, or
vaguely international food, and eating at McDonald's felt like a
square meal.

Now the tide is turning, and especially in the Baltics,
restaurants are proudly serving local specialities again. Try the
mushroom soup in Estonia, the smoked peas with bacon in
Latvia, and the zeppelin dumplings in Lithuania.

Restaurants

Despite rising prices, you can eat a satisfying restaurant meal in
any of these cities for $5–$15 a person. Unless the bill includes
a service charge, it's common to round things up or leave a
small tip (no more than 5–10 percent).

Finding good restaurants is easy in the Baltics, but a
problem in Russia. Just because something says "restaurant"
or "café" doesn't mean you want to eat there. Check the
menu carefully. It is still possible to stand in a long line and
pay pennies' worth of rubles to eat gagging, lukewarm food
at stand-up tables in a dimly lit, filthy café with puddles of
tracked-in rainwater on the floor. And it's easy to eat
mediocre $20 meals at proudly exclusive restaurants with
offensive doormen, sleazy variety shows, thick-walleted customers with dark glasses, and waiters who pretend it's
absolutely natural to pay 20 bucks for dinner in this part of
the world. For the best value, use the listings in this guidebook and the advice of your hotel or hostel manager.

When in search of a bathroom in a restaurant, remember: A downward-pointing triangle means "men," an upward-
pointing triangle means "women." (Think "missionary
position.")

Picnics

Small grocery stores and, to a lesser degree, supermarkets
have sprouted all over the Baltics and Russia in the past three
to four years and buying food is no problem now. Especially
in Riga and St. Petersburg you can also head to the farmer's
market for the best selection of cheese, sausage, and fresh

fruits and vegetables. Russian bread is particularly good—look for the dark, heavy brown loaves which Russians call black (*chorny*, чёрный) bread. Food prices in Russia equal, and often exceed, prices in America, largely because so many of the groceries on sale in Moscow and St. Petersburg are imported. Baltic food prices are lower.

Water
If you want to stay absolutely on the safe side, drink only boiled or filtered water, soft drinks, tea, and juice. This is especially true in St. Petersburg, where a parasite called giardia infests the water system. It causes upset stomach and diarrhea, but can be eradicated with a prescription drug called *Flagyl* (metronidazole). Most visitors to St. Petersburg don't get sick, and if you avoid unboiled St. Petersburg water you should be OK, too. We brush with St. Petersburg water and just don't swallow.

How do Russians get by?
Russian salaries have not kept pace with food prices, so how do people eat? Why aren't they starving—especially the elderly, subsisting on a monthly inflation-squeezed pension check, their savings soaked away by the ruble's swift decline? This can be hard to understand on a quick visit, since you're isolated from the channels that Russians use to get by. To start with, housing and transport are subsidized, so a larger percentage of one's salary can be spent on food. Many people do part- or full-time work that doesn't show up in official salary statistics, and get extra income from renting an extra apartment or selling a car. As for the elderly, most live with extended families. When their children are at work and their grandchildren at school, pensioners have the time to stand in line for the cheapest (albeit lowest-quality) groceries from state-run stores, or to find the very best bargains at the private farmer's markets. Many Russians are lucky enough to own or have access to a *dacha* (country home), where they spend warm weekends planting, picking, canning, and preserving fruit and vegetables to hoard through the long winters. These are their secrets of survival.

Safety and Health
Though crime has increased vastly since Communist times, Russia and the Baltics are still far safer than New York City.

The situation in the Baltics is comparable to other European countries. In Russia, crime is coarser, cruder, and less professional than in America, often just a fight picked on the street or the drunken thuggery of unemployed young men. The Russian Mafia is interested in businesses and longterm residents, not tourists. Street kids can be a problem, especially at train stations and in Moscow. They'll try to reach into your pockets. Shoo them away forcefully.

Use the same precautions you would at home or anywhere else in Europe: don't flaunt wealth, keep valuables in your money belt, avoid dark alleys, and don't talk back to drunks. Don't speak English loudly in public, and try not to draw attention to your foreignness.

Trains are generally safe, but it's wise to take some simple precautions. Women traveling by train may be able to get permission from the conductor to switch seats into a compartment with other women. You can lock the compartment door with the metal flip lock. For extra security, stuff a wad of paper, a cork, or a cut-off film canister into the cavity of the flip lock so that it can't be jimmied from the outside. Some people even tie down the door handle with a length of cord.

Ultimately, you are less at risk from criminals than from dilapidation, decay, and corrupt law enforcement. The scariest things we've had to deal with personally in Russia have been falling glass, loose manhole covers, and arbitrary cops and customs officers. The local police are not renowned for their quick response or helpfulness. (Emergency numbers in Russia and the Baltics are: 01 for fire, 02 for the police, 03 for an ambulance.)

As for health, elementary precautions are in order, but paranoia is unnecessary. Watch what you eat and drink. Avoid dubious meat and be careful about eating street food. Make sure your shots are up to date. If you're going to be in Eastern Europe for a few months, talk to your doctor. Take a basic first-aid kit and any special medicines you may need. Distrust local hospitals—if you have serious problems, consult your embassy for a referral to a Western doctor, or head to Finland.

Surviving Russia

As conditions in the Baltic states diverge further and further from those in Russia, it becomes more difficult to write a unified introduction to the entire area. In 1993, when we wrote the first edition of this book, the same advice about post-Soviet eating, sleeping, and transportation applied regardless of whether you were in Lithuania or Leningrad. By 1996, the Baltic states had become "normal" European countries, and Americans could travel from Helsinki to Warsaw without a visa, but travel in Russia stayed substantially the same.

We face a special dilemma in trying to write about Russia. On the one hand, world-famous icons of culture and history, such as the Hermitage in St. Petersburg and the Kremlin in Moscow, ought to be described with the reverence they deserve. On the other, one has to admit that much of Russian life is ugly and frustrating. Not long ago a visit to St. Petersburg led a journalist for London's *Sunday Times* to remark that the country's "rudeness and illogicality . . . makes social life in such a place a horror only marginally preferable to burning for eternity in hell."

That is an extreme statement, but almost every Westerner in Russia feels this way sometimes. Moscow *is* one of the great cities of the world—but as such it has more in common with Beijing and Mexico City than with New York and Paris. By Western standards, Russia first disappoints, then maddens, and finally saddens. It is racked by ecological devastation and economic hopelessness. Life in Moscow and St. Petersburg is as expensive as the West and as squalid as much of the Third World, and the weather, scenery, and cuisine are better elsewhere.

Then why visit? Well, Russia is, in places, breathtakingly lovely. In other places, it is awesome. (Standing in front of the Stalin-era skyscrapers in Moscow, one cannot help but feel both fear and respect.) And though public life on the streets in Russia is difficult, individual people, especially inside their own apartments, are warm and giving. In museums, churches, and concert halls, Russia's cultural and artistic heritage survives.

And Russia is extremely important—to recent history, to the present, and to the future of the world. It is important to see and understand the evil that the Soviet system perpetrated on its people, in the same way as it is important to learn about the Holocaust. This is a country where millions of innocent people died under Communism, and where the state poisoned the lives of those who survived.

Although we have listed plenty of museums and typical sightseeing attractions in this book, it would be a great waste to visit Moscow and see only the "sights" such as St. Basil's and the Kremlin. Do see the sights, but also stand in line for suburban train tickets, shop in average stores for a picnic lunch, and take the Metro during rush hour. You will get more out of your trip if you consider yourself not a tourist but a student and an explorer. Yes, you must step through puddles, avoid open manholes, crowd onto escalators, search hard for a decent place to eat, and talk to many unfriendly people through tiny holes in large windows—but we think it's worth it.

Stranger in a Strange Land

We travel all the way to Europe to enjoy differences—to become temporary locals. You'll experience frustrations. Certain truths that we find "God-given" or "self-evident," like cold beer, ice in drinks, bottomless cups of coffee, hot showers, body odor smelling bad, and bigger being better, are suddenly not so true. One of the benefits of travel is the eye-opening realization that there are logical, civil, and even better alternatives. A willingness to go local ensures that you'll enjoy a full dose of European hospitality.

If there is a negative aspect to the European image of Americans, we are big, loud, aggressive, impolite, rich, and a bit naive. While Europeans look bemusedly at some of our Yankee excesses—and worriedly at others—they nearly always afford us individual travelers all the warmth we deserve.

Back Door Manners

While updating this book, we heard over and over again that our readers are considerate and fun to have as guests. Thank you for traveling as temporary locals who are sensitive to the culture. It's fun to follow you in our travels.

Send Us a Postcard, Drop Us a Line

If you enjoy a successful trip with the help of this book and would like to share your discoveries, please send any tips, recommendations, criticisms, or corrections to us at Europe Through the Back Door, Box 2009, Edmonds, WA 98020. We personally read and value all feedback. Tips actually used may get you a first-class railpass in heaven.

For our latest travel information, tap into our web site: http://www.ricksteves.com, or find us on America Online (key word: Rick Steves). Our E-mail address is ricksteves@aol.com. Anyone is welcome to request a free issue of our Back Door quarterly newsletter (it's free anyway).

Judging from all the positive feedback and happy postcards we receive from travelers who have used this book, it's safe to assume you're on your way to a great vacation—independent, inexpensive, and with the finesse of an experienced traveler.

Thanks, and happy travels!

BACK DOOR TRAVEL PHILOSOPHY
As Taught in *Rick Steves' Europe Through the Back Door*

Travel is intensified living—maximum thrills per minute and one of the last great sources of legal adventure. Travel is freedom. It's recess, and we need it. Experiencing the real world requires catching it by surprise, going casual . . . "Through the Back Door."

Affording travel is a matter of priorities. (Make do with the old car.) You can travel—simply, safely, and comfortably—just about anywhere in the world for $60 a day plus transportation costs. In many ways, spending more money only builds a thicker wall between you and what you came to see. The world is a cultural carnival, and time after time, you'll find that its best acts are free and the best seats are the cheap ones.

A tight budget forces you to travel close to the ground, meeting and communicating with the people, not relying on service with a purchased smile. Never sacrifice sleep, nutrition, safety, or cleanliness in the name of budget. Simply enjoy the local-style alternatives to expensive hotels and restaurants.

Extroverts have more fun. If your trip is low on magic moments, kick yourself and make things happen. If you don't enjoy a place, maybe you don't know enough about it. Seek the truth. Recognize tourist traps. Give a culture the benefit of your open mind. See things as different, but not better or worse. Any culture has much to share.

Of course, travel, like the world, is a series of hills and valleys. Be fanatically positive and militantly optimistic. If something's not to your liking, change your liking. Travel is addicting. It can make you a happier American as well as a citizen of the world. Our Earth is home to nearly 6 billion equally important people. It's humbling to travel and find that people don't envy Americans. They like us, but with all due respect, they wouldn't trade passports.

Globe-trotting destroys ethnocentricity. It helps you understand and appreciate different cultures. Travel changes people. It broadens perspectives and teaches new ways to measure quality of life. Many travelers toss aside their hometown blinders. Their prized souvenirs are the strands of different cultures they decide to knit into their own character. The world is a cultural yarn shop. And Back Door travelers are weaving the ultimate tapestry. Come on, join in!

GETTING YOUR VISA

No More Baltic Visas

Americans no longer need a visa to enter *any* of the three Baltic states as a tourist. Just like going to England, Italy, or Sweden, all you need is your passport. For those who do require a Baltic visa, such as Canadians visiting Latvia, getting one is a simple matter of sending your passport to the nearest consulate with a single form and a small fee. (For the Latvian embassy in Ottawa call 613/238-6868.) Canadians enter Lithuania and Estonia visa-free.

Russian Visas

Getting your Russian visa isn't hard, but it takes a few weeks of pre-trip planning. Not only does Russia require visas for foreign tourists, they require you to present an official letter from a sponsoring organization in Russia. In other words, whereas getting a visa for most countries in the world simply means presenting your passport at the consulate and paying for a stamp, to visit Russia you also need to give the consulate a "visa support letter" from a Russian organization, which technically commits that organization to taking responsibility for you while you're in Russia. For some tourists, this organization is the travel agency or tour operator who is arranging your trip; for independent travelers, it is usually a hotel or hostel where you'll be staying for part of your journey. This means that you have a special relationship with this hotel. You're not a free agent; you don't just call up and say "Hi, I'm coming on the 25th." Rather, you make a commitment to them, and in return they give you a piece of paper which makes it all OK with the men in blue.

Getting Started

First send a self-addressed, stamped envelope to the nearest of the Russian consulates listed at the end of this section, with a request for visa application forms and instructions (or use their fax-back service at 800/634-4296). Fill out the English side of the application. For most readers of this book, the object of your journey will be "tourism." Under dates of travel, you might add a few days at the beginning and the end of your trip, just for flexibility. Leave the line about "Index and name of your tourist group" and the medical coverage line blank. Collect three passport-size photographs, and make a photocopy of the first page of your passport.

You won't need to send in your passport, because a Russian visa is not a passport stamp, but rather a piece of colored paper folded into three sections. The first section is your entry (въезд) visa, which is torn off by the border guard as you enter the country. The middle section is blank-backed for registration stamps. The last section is your exit (выезд) visa, which, together with the middle page, is taken away by the guard as you leave the country. The next step before you send in your application is to get a visa support letter.

Visa Support Sources

If you plan to stay at the **St. Petersburg International Hostel**, the easiest thing to do is contact their American office: Russian Youth Hostels & Tourism, 409 N. Pacific Coast Highway #106, Suite 390, Redondo Beach, California 90277 (301/379-4316; fax 379-8420). They'll take all your paperwork, deal with the consulate and send back your completed visa. Nobody else in Russia is so able to combine a low per-night price with efficient visa support from American and European offices. See the St. Petersburg accommodations section for more details. They take bookings for several other hostels in Russia and the Travellers Guest House in Moscow. Like most organizations, the International Hostel will give you a visa that is valid for slightly longer than you plan to stay at the hostel, so that you can travel elsewhere or visit friends; but be sure to ask them to do this.

The next best way to get visa support is from organizations in Russia that can book accommodations for you and fax you a visa support letter, but leave it to you to submit everything to the consulate. **Peter T.I.P.S**, a tourist office in St. Petersburg, is one such organization (see the St. Petersburg section). Other outfits that have been relatively successful are the **Host Family Association,** which sets up homestays with families in St. Petersburg for $50–60 per day for two people, $100 with all meals (tel./fax 7/812/275-1992 in St. Petersburg, E-mail alexei@hofak.hop.stu.neva.ru), and **White Nights,** which arranges hotels and homestays in St. Petersburg and Moscow (St. Louis office tel./fax 314/991-5512, E-mail russiawnight@rcom.sbb.su, or on the Web at http://www.

concourse.net/bus/wnights/. The **Russia Experience** also provides homestays in St. Petersburg and Moscow (U.S.A. contact: Petit Travel Consultants, tel. 800/683-7403, fax 508/792-0065). In theory any Russian hotel should be able to issue you visa support in this way, but except for the most expensive places, most are not very adept at dealing with foreigners traveling independently.

Another way to get visa support is simply to pay a Russian organization to go to the trouble of sending you a visa support letter even though you may have nothing more to do with them. **IRO Travel** at the Travellers Guest House in Moscow will do this for you (see the Moscow section). When you arrive in Russia, you'll need to have the organization that issued the letter register you with OVIR (see below). This means a trip to the organization's office and sometimes leaving your passport and visa with them for a day or two.

If you have friends in Russia, they can mail you a so-called "private" visa invitation slip that they get from their local OVIR office (see below). This serves as your visa support letter, and you should write "private visit" on your application instead of "tourism." You can also get visa support letters from Russian companies, institutions, and other organizations outside the travel industry; in this case you should probably put down "business" on your application as the purpose of your trip. Finally, if you have a cross-Russia train ticket (like on the Trans-Siberian), the ticket serves as your visa support and the purpose of your trip is "transit." Transit visas are less desirable since they limit your time in Russia.

Sending In The Visa Application

With your visa support in hand, you're almost there. Assemble your application; your three photographs; the photocopy of the front page of your passport; and your visa support letter. Make out another self-addressed, stamped envelope. Type up a cover letter; it could just say "Enclosed please find all the materials for my visa application." Write a $40 check to the consulate for their standard two-week turnaround, and send everything off to them. (If you want your visa faster, they'll be happy to take more of your money.)

We're all hoping that Russia will simplify their visa requirements. There's nothing unusual about having to get special permission from a country before you're allowed to

visit. But it *is* unusual to require people to get an official spon-
sor for their trip. It dates from an era when travelers were
always affiliated with a state-run organization rather than
responsible for themselves. It also encourages abuse, since independent visitors are in effect simply paying their sponsoring
organization for an official letter and a signature. Unfortunately the Russian Foreign Ministry hasn't seemed to realize
that the best way to reform the system is to eliminate the spon-
sorship and invitation requirement, at least for short visits by
tourists from wealthier countries, who aren't likely to try to
settle in Russia. This is the way most countries handle visas.
And it would also be a big boost to the Russian travel and
tourism industry. But in Russia there is a tendency for bureau-
cracy to be organized in exactly the opposite way from what
might seem most sensible to Americans, and getting a visa is
your first chance to get used to this. There may also be an ele-
ment of pride involved. For a Russian, getting a Western visa
is a long and humiliating process; if Russia issued visas to
Westerners any more quickly, the imbalance might seem
incompatible with Russia's perceived "greatness."

Notes on Russian Visas

A normal single-entry visa is valid for one entry and one exit
at any time between the dates listed on it. It is possible to get
multiple-entry Russian visas, but it's a lot of extra hassle and
money (ask Russian Youth Hostels & Tourism if you're serious). Instead, structure your trip so that you only pass
through Russia once.

Foreigners can travel almost anywhere in Russia now,
although visas still have a "destination" line which sometimes
lists just one or two cities.

You can get your visa from any Russian consulate in the
world. The application procedure is roughly similar, though
every consulate has peculiar mutations. Also, you don't have to
get your visa by mail; if you live nearby, you can just bring everything to the consulate and come back in a couple weeks to pick
up your visa.

Once you have your visa and are in Russia, you can of
course stay at any hotel in the country regardless of whether it is
set up to offer foreigners visa support or not. For example, there
are plenty of old Soviet hotels in St. Petersburg and Moscow
with shoddy (but usually acceptable) rooms and high (but usually

not outrageous) prices. They're rarely used to dealing with independent travelers and they aren't good at sending visa support letters overseas, but if you call up and ask for a room they will quite likely say yes. However, we strongly advise setting up all your accommodations in Russia in advance from the United States.

Group Tours and Packages

Russia is one place where a group tour or a package can make sense. The organizers do all the hard work for you—visa processing and registration, hotel reservations, and transfers. We can recommend two tour operators, and you can ask your travel agent about others. In 1996 EuroCruises offered a two-night trip to St. Petersburg, starting in Helsinki, for $525 per person including round-trip train fare, double-occupancy in a good hotel, breakfasts, transfers, and sightseeing (tel. 800/688-3876). Finnair has had good airfare-plus-hotel packages departing from New York (tel. 800/950-5000).

Registering Your Visa

You'll notice that your Russian visa says "every person is required to register his passport within three days after his arrival in the destination point with the exception of holidays and days off." Only travelers on transit visas are exempt from registration.

The organization that issued your visa support letter is responsible for registration when you arrive in Russia. Make sure that the people who give you your visa support letter tell you where, when, and by whom your visa will be registered. Registration consists of a stamp on the white page of your visa by the state Visa and Registration Authority (known as OVIR, which rhymes with "severe"). OVIR permits some organizations, particularly hotels, to have their own stamps on the premises so they don't have to come to the office every day. In fact, any Russian hotel you stay in may stamp your visa even if they have no connection with your inviting organization.

Registration used to be a way of keeping tabs on visiting foreigners. But since restrictions on internal travel were eliminated in 1991, registration has become an entirely pointless bureaucratic exercise. Without going into all the gory details, let's just say that the system is too absurd and cumbersome to be perfectly comprehensible or perfectly enforceable. In practice, you should make sure that the organization that invited you registers you. Although you can try to have this done within three days of your arrival, probably no one will care if you are late. Most important, *make sure that your visa gets stamped at least once before you leave Russia.* It matters little where. Leaving Russia with an unstamped visa is a fifty-fifty proposition. They might not notice; if they do notice, they might not care; if they do care, the border guards might only extort a $50–$200 "fine" from you, but they could prevent you from leaving the country.

Extending Your Russian Visa

Avoid extending your Russian visa. The only way to prolong your stay in Russia is to have the organization that invited you apply to OVIR for an extension, an often unsuccessful process which includes bringing your passport and writing an official letter using various stock phrases such as "The matter will be dealt with according to the established protocol." You are not allowed to deal with OVIR yourself. Rules, fees, and extension lengths differ from one OVIR to the next and from one month to the next.

Leaving Russia with an expired visa is a major sin. Don't do it. While crossing the border at 2:00 a.m. on a visa that expired at midnight is likely to be overlooked, and one or two days' lateness could prompt a fine, anything longer than that and you may simply not be let out of the country. If this happens, it is possible to obtain a special "exit visa" from OVIR. Ask for help from the organization that originally invited you. If all else fails, contact your consulate.

Currency Declarations

When you enter Russia, you should be given a small form for declaring how much foreign currency you are carrying. Make sure that you fill out this form (it's called a *deklaratsiya* or декларация); make sure it gets stamped by one of the customs officers, and keep it safe so that you can surrender it when you exit Russia. Under communism, the purpose of the declaration was to prevent you from depleting the Soviet Union's scarce foreign exchange reserves, and on leaving Russia the customs service can still confiscate currency in excess of what you declared when you entered—despite the fact that there are now ATMs in Moscow where you can withdraw money from your American bank account! One of the reasons the declarations are still in use may be to enrich the pockets of the customs officers who "fine" exiting travelers who either lost their *deklaratsiya*, or were never given one from the start.

Russian Consulates in the U.S.A.
For an application, send an SASE, or use the fax-back service at 800/634-4296. People in the know say that the Russian consulate in New York can be a stickler for details, whereas the San Francisco consulate is the most friendly and lenient.

New York: 9 E. 91st St., New York, NY 10128. This consulate, open Monday–Friday 9:30–12:30, has a useful information number, 212/348-0779, with a helpful recording giving complete details on the visa process. To talk to a real person, call 212/348-0926 (fax 831-9162).

Washington, DC: 1825 Phelps Place NW, Washington, DC 20008, tel. 202/939-8903, fax 483-7579.

Seattle: 2323 Westin Building, 2001 6th Ave. Seattle, WA 98121, tel. 206/728-1910, fax 728-1871.

San Francisco: 2790 Green St., San Francisco, CA 94123, tel. 415/929-0862, fax 929-0306.

The Russian Consulate in Helsinki
The Helsinki consulate is a convenient place to get your visa processed if you're going to be spending any time in Finland. The Russian diplomatic complex in Helsinki occupies an entire city block next to the "Kaivopuisto" stop of trams 3B and 3T (if you're coming south on 3B, it's the stop after the last ferry terminal). You can also walk from the center of town. The consular entrance is at Vuorimiehenkatu 6 (tel. 661 449), near the corner of Ullankatu on the other side of the complex from the tram. By Russian standards it's extremely efficient, and English is spoken. One-week processing costs 100mk, two- to three-day processing costs 300mk (exchange rate: 4.5 mk = $1). Show them a Trans-Siberian ticket and they'll normally outfit you with a ten-day transit visa, which costs the same. Standard paperwork is required (Monday–Friday 9:30–12:00, but get there at 9:00 for a good spot in line; the sign that says the consulate opens at 10:00 is wrong).

GATEWAYS TO THE BALTICS AND RUSSIA: HELSINKI, STOCKHOLM, AND WARSAW

Here are some tips to help you make it smoothly through the transportation and bureaucratic hoops you'll encounter if you use Helsinki, Stockholm, or Warsaw as a gateway to the Baltics and Russia.

Helsinki is just a cruise away from Stockholm. To help you out, we've included a pared-down version of the Helsinki chapter from *Rick Steves' Scandinavia 1997*.

HELSINKI

Helsinki feels close to Russia. It is. Much of it reminds me of St. Petersburg. It's no wonder Hollywood chose to film *Dr. Zhivago*, *Reds*, and *Gorky Park* here. (They filmed the Moscow Railway Station scenes in *Dr. Zhivago* in the low red-brick building near the Viking Terminal.) There is a huge and impressive Russian Orthodox church overlooking the harbor, a large Russian community, and several fine Russian restaurants.

In the early 1800s, when the Russians took Finland from Sweden, they moved the capital eastward from Turku, making Helsinki the capital of their "autonomous duchy." I asked a woman in the tourist office if a particular café was made for Russian officers. In a rare spasm of candor (this was during the Cold War), she said, "All of 19th-century Helsinki was made for Russian officers."

Today Helsinki is gray and green. A little windy and cold, it looks like it's stuck somewhere in the north near the Russian border. But it makes the best of its difficult situation and will leave you impressed and glad to have dropped in. Start with the two-hour "Hello, Helsinki" bus tour that meets the boat at the dock. Enjoy Helsinki's ruddy harborfront market, count goosebumps in her churches, and dive into Finnish culture in the open-air folk museum.

Europe's most neoclassical city has many architectural overleafs, and it tends to turn guests into fans of town planning and architecture. Buildings, designs, fashions, and people fit sensitively into their surroundings. Dissimilar elements are fused into a complex but comfortable whole. It's a very intimate and human place.

Planning Your Time

Allow a day for Helsinki. Take the orientation bus tour upon arrival, mingle through the market, buy and eat a picnic, and drop by the TI. People-watch and browse through downtown to the National Museum. For the afternoon, choose between the National Museum, the Open-Air Folk Museum, or a harbor boat tour. Relax over a cup of coffee in the Café Kappeli.

Orientation

(4.5 mk = $1, tel. code in Finland: 09, tel. code from outside Finland: 358-9)

Helsinki is a colorful shopping town of 500,000 people. The compact city center is a great area to roam—perfect for a brisk walk.

Tourist Information: Helsinki has TIs at the boat terminals, inside the train station, and (closest to the ferries) on the market square (market square office open weekdays 9:00–19:00, weekends 9:00–15:00, shorter hours off-season, tel. 169 3757 or 174 088, fax 169 3839). The TIs are uniformly friendly, helpful, well stocked in brochures, and blond. Pick up the city map, the "Route Map" (public transit), "Helsinki on Foot" (six well-described and mapped walking tours), and the monthly *Helsinki This Week* magazine which lists sights, hours, and events. *City* magazine is geared for the younger crowd. Ask about the 3T tourist tram and go over your sightseeing plans.

Travel Agency: A handy travel agency specializing in ferry reservations out of Helsinki is Atlas Cruising Center/Merelle-Till Havs (Monday–Friday 9:00–17:00, Saturday 10:00–14:00, Kluuvikatu 6, tel. 651-011, fax 636-786).

Getting Around Helsinki

By Bus and Tram: With the public transit route map and a little mental elbow grease, the buses and trams are easy, giving you the city by the tail. Tickets (9 mk) are good for an hour of travel and are purchased from the driver. The tourist tram, 3T, makes the rounds of most of the town's major sights, letting you stop and go for 9 mk an hour. The TI has a helpful explanatory brochure (not available on the bus).

The Tourist Ticket (25 mk for 24 hours of unlimited

travel) pays if you take three or more rides. The Helsinki Card
(105 mk) gives you free entry to city sights and use of all buses
and trams for 24 hours. In summer the special red "Pub Tram"
makes a 40-minute loop through the city while its passengers
get looped on the one beer which comes with the 25 mk ticket
(hourly 11:00–15:00 from Mikaelsgata near the train station).

By Bike: Greenbike rents bikes at Mannerheimtie 13,
across from the Parliament House.

Do-It-Yourself "Welcome to Helsinki" Walk

Start at the harbor. The colorful produce market on the market square thrives daily 7:00–14:00 and 15:30–20:00 (closed
Saturday afternoon and sometimes on Sunday). At the head
of the harbor, facing the cruise ships, this is Helsinki's center. Don't miss the busy two-tone red-brick indoor market
hall. Across the street you'll see the City Tourist Office.
Drop in to ask questions. The round door next to the TI
leads into the delightful Jugendsalen. Designed, apparently,
by a guy named Art Nouveau, this free and pleasant information center for locals offers interesting historical exhibits, a
knockout art deco interior, and a public WC (Monday–
Friday 9:00–18:00, Sunday 12:00–18:00, closed Saturday;
Pohjoisesplanadi 19). One block inland behind the tourist
office are the fine neoclassical Senate Square and the
Lutheran Cathedral.

Across the street from the TI, in the park facing the
square, is my favorite café in northern Europe, the Café Kappeli. When you've got some time, dip into this turn-of-the-
century gazebo-like oasis of coffee, pastry, and relaxation. Built
in the 19th century, it was a popular hangout for local intellec-
tuals and artists.

Behind the café runs the entertaining park, sandwiched
between the north and south Esplanadi—Helsinki's top shopping
boulevard. Walk it. The north (tourist office) side is interesting
for window shopping, people-watching, and sun-worshiping.
The huge Academic Bookstore, designed by Alvar Aalto (nearby
at 1 Keskuskatu), has a great map and travel guide section and
café. Finally you'll come to the prestigious Stockman's department store—Finland's Harrod's. Just beyond is the main intersection in town, Esplanadi and Mannerheimintie. Nearby you'll
see the famous *Three Blacksmiths* statue. (Locals say, "If a virgin
walks by, they'll strike the anvil." It doesn't work. I tried.)

A block to the right, through a busy shopping center, is the harsh (in a serene way) architecture of the central train station, designed by Eliel Saarinen in 1916. Wander around inside. Continuing past the Posti and the statue, return to Mannerheimintie, which leads to the large white Finlandia Hall, another Aalto masterpiece. While it's not normally open, there are often two tours a day in the summer (ask at the TI). Across the street is the excellent little Finnish National Museum, and a few blocks behind that is the sit-down-and-wipe-a-tear beautiful rock church, Temppeliaukio. Sit. Enjoy the music. It's a wonderful place to end this walk.

From nearby Arkadiankatu Street, bus #24 will take you to the Sibelius monument in a lovely park. The same ticket is good on a later #24. Ride to the end of the line—the bridge to the Seurasaari island and Finland's open-air folk museum. From here, bus #24 returns to the Esplanadi.

Sights—Helsinki

▲▲▲**Orientation Bus Tour**—A fast, very good two-hour introductory tour leaves daily around 9:30 from both the Viking and Silja terminals after the ships dock from Stockholm. The rapid-fire two- or three-language tour costs 90 mk and gives a good historic overview—a look at all the important buildings from the newly-remodeled Olympic Stadium to embassy row, with too-fast ten-minute stops at the Lutheran Cathedral, the Sibelius monument, and the Church in the Rock (Temppeliaukio).

If you're on a tight budget and don't care to get the general overview of Helsinki, you can do the essence of this tour on your own as explained in my city walk (above). The tour drops you off at the market square, near the National Museum (if you ask), or at your hotel by 11:30.

If you'd like more time in the Church of the Rock, leave the tour there and consider walking 3 blocks to the National Museum and the Finlandia Hall.

There is a shorter, cheaper tour that's nearly as good (70 mk and included on the Helsinki Card, daily in summer at 11:30 and 13:30, from the train station or near the TI at 10:30, 12:30, and 14:30, tel. 588 5166, no stop at the Lutheran Cathedral), but I like the "pick you up at the boat and drop you at your hotel or back on the market square" efficiency of the 9:30 tour. Buy your ticket on board or at the tourist desk in the terminal (availability no problem).

▲▲**Lutheran Cathedral**—With its prominent green dome overlooking the city and harbor, this church is the masterpiece of Carl Ludwig Engel. Open the pew gate and sit to savor neo-classical nirvana. Finished in 1852, the interior is pure architectural truth (9:00–18:00, Sunday 12:00–20:00, shorter hours in winter).

Senate Square—From the top of the steps of the Lutheran Cathedral, study Europe's finest neoclassical square. The Senate building is on your left. The small blue stone building with the slanted mansard roof in the far left corner is from 1757, one of just two pre-Russian conquest buildings remaining in Helsinki. On the right is the University building. Czar Alexander II, a friend of Finland's, is honored by the statue in the square.

▲▲**Uspensky Russian Orthodox Cathedral**—Hovering above the market square, blessing the harbor, and facing the Lutheran Cathedral as Russian culture faces Europe's, is a fine icon experience and western Europe's largest Russian Orthodox church (daily 9:30–16:00, except Tuesday 9:30–18:00).

▲▲▲**Temppeliaukio Church**—Another great piece of church architecture, this was blasted out of solid rock and capped with a copper and skylight dome. It's normally filled with live or recorded music and awestruck visitors. I almost cried. Another form of simple truth, it's impossible to describe. Grab a pew. Gawk upward at a 14-mile-long coil of copper wire. Look at the bull's-eye and ponder God. Forget your camera. Just sit in the middle, ignore the crowds, and be thankful for peace—under your feet is an air raid shelter that can accommodate 6,000 people. (Open Monday–Saturday 10:00–20:00, Sunday 12:00–13:45 and 15:15–17:45.) To experience the church in action, attend the Lutheran English service (Sunday at 14:00, tel. 494698) or one of the many concerts.

▲**Sibelius Monument**—Six hundred stainless steel pipes shimmer over a rock in a park to honor Finland's greatest composer. Notice the face of Sibelius (which the artist was forced to add to silence the critics of this abstract work). Bus #24 stops here (or catch a quick glimpse on the left from the bus) on its way to the Open-Air Folk Museum. The 3T tram, which runs more frequently, stops a few blocks away. By the way, music lovers enjoy the English language tours of the slick new Finnish National Opera (closed in July).

▲**Seurasaari Open-Air Folk Museum**—Inspired by

Stockholm's Skansen, also on a lovely island on the edge of
town, this is a collection of 100 historic buildings gathered
from every corner of Finland. Many of the buildings are staffed
with an information person 11:00–17:00. It's wonderfully fur-
nished and gives rushed visitors a great opportunity to sample
the far reaches of Finland without leaving the capital city. Buy
the 10 mk guidebook. (The park is free, 15 mk to enter the
buildings, daily June–August 11:00–17:00; May and September
Monday–Friday 9:00–15:00, Saturday and Sunday
11:00–17:00). In winter the museum is almost not worth a
look; the park is open but the buildings are closed. Ride bus
#24 to the end of the line and walk across the quaint foot-
bridge. Call or check at the TI for English tour (usually at
11:30 and 15:30) and evening folk dance schedules (usually
Tuesday, Thursday, and Sunday at 19:00, tel. 484712).

▲▲**National Museum**—This is a pleasant, easy-to-handle
collection (covering Finland's story from A to Z with good
English descriptions) in a grand building designed by three of
Finland's greatest early architects. The highlight is the Finno-
Ugric exhibit downstairs, well-explained by the 20-page English booklet (15 mk, Wednesday–Sunday 11:00–17:00, Tuesday
11:00–20:00, closed Monday, closes one hour earlier off-
season; across the street from the Finlandia Hall, tel. 40501).
The museum café has light meals and Finnish treats such as
lingonberry juice and reindeer quiche.

Finlandia Hall—Alvar Aalto's most famous building in his
native Finland means little to the non-architect without a tour
(20 mk, all summer, noon and 14:00, tel. 40241).

▲**Harbor tours**—Several boat companies line the market
square offering 90-minute, 60-mk cruises around the waterfront nearly every hour 10:00–17:30. The narration is slow-
moving and in three languages, but if the weather's good and
you're looking for something one step above a snooze in the
park, it's a nice break. Gluttons can try IHA-Lines Cruises
from market square—if you eat the equivalent of your fare's
worth on board, the ride is free (if the company stays in
business).

▲**Flea Market**—Hietalahti Market, Finland's biggest flea
market, is particularly interesting, with the many Russian and
Baltic people hawking whatever they can—from bearskin hats
to Soviet wing medals—for a little hard currency (Monday–
Saturday 8:00–14:00, summer evenings Monday–Friday

15:30–21:00). If you brake for garage sales, it's well worth the 15-minute walk from the harbor.

Suomenlinna—The "fortified island" is a 20-minute ferry or water bus ride (18 mk–22 mk round-trip, on the half hour) from the market square. The old fort is now a popular park with several museums.

Sauna—Finland's vaporized fountain of youth is the sauna. Public saunas are a dying breed these days, since saunas are standard equipment in nearly every Finnish apartment and home. Your boat or hotel has a sauna. Your youth hostel probably even has one. For a real experience, ask about the Finnish Sauna Society (70 mk, bus #20 for 20 minutes, in a park on the waterfront, men-only most nights, Thursday is women's night). For a cheap and easy public sauna, go to the Olympic swimming pool at the Olympic Stadium (10 mk, pool and sauna open 7:00–20:00 except Sunday 9:00–20:00).

Nightlife—Remember that Finland was the first country to give women the vote. The sexes are equal in the bars and on the dance floor. Finns are easily approachable and tourists are not a headache to the locals (as they are in places like Paris and Munich). While it's easy to make friends, anything alcoholic is very expensive. For the latest on hot night spots, read the English insert of the *City* magazine that lists the "Best" of everything in Helsinki. For very cheap fun, Hietaranta beach is where the local kids hang out (and even skinny-dip) at 22:00 or 23:00. This city is one of Europe's safest after dark.

Sleeping in Helsinki
(4.5 mk = about $1, tel. code from outside of Finland: 358-9)

Standard budget hotel doubles start at $100. But there are many special deals, and dorm and hostel alternatives. You have four basic budget options—cheap youth hostels, student dorms turned "summer hotels," plain and basic low-class hotels, or expensive business-class hotels at a special summer or weekend clearance sale rate.

Summer (mid-June to mid-August) is "off-season" in Helsinki, as are Friday, Saturday, and Sunday nights the rest of the year. You can arrive in the morning and expect to find a budget room. In the train station next to Track 4 (a pleasant 20-minute walk from the boat docks, or tram 3B from Silja, bus #13 from Viking, on arrival only) is the **Hotellikeskus** room-finding service (June–August 9:00–19:00, Sunday

10:00–18:00; off-season 10:00–17:00 Monday–Friday only).
For 12 mk, they'll book you a bed in the price range of your
choice. They know what wild bargains are available. Consider
a luxury hotel clearance deal, which may cost $20 more than
the cheapies. Ask about any Helsinki card "specials," which
lower prices mid-June to early September and on weekends.
Their 12 mk fee is reasonable, but they're happy to do the job
over the phone for free. Call from the harbor or Stockholm
(tel. 09/171133).

Sleeping in Classy "Real" Hotels

Hotel Anna, plush and very central, is one of the best values
in town (single-330 mk, double-430 mk in summer with breakfast and private showers; near Mannerheimintie and Esplanadi,
a 15-minute walk from the boat; 1 Annankatu, tel. 616 621, fax
602 664).

Hotel Cumulus Olympia is often about the least expensive hotel in town (double-365 mk in summer with private
showers and breakfast; not so central but on the 3B or #1 tram
line at the Sport Hall stop, 2 Lantinen Brahenkatu, tel. 69151,
fax 691 5219). Hotels Anna and Olympia both charge 600 mk
during business season.

Hotel Arthur, a five-minute walk from the train station
and Senate Square, has spacious rooms (single-330 mk–395
mk, double with bath-400 mk–495 mk; accepts Visa, Master-
Card, American Express; Vuorikatu 17, 00100 Helsinki, tel.
173 441, fax 626 880).

Sleeping in Hostels

Eurohostel is an upscale, modern hostel located a block from
the Viking terminal or a ten-minute walk from the market
square (single-175 mk, double-230 mk, triple-345 mk, including
sheets, private lockable closets, and morning sauna, less 15 mk
per person with hostel cards; breakfast-28 mk; doubles and
triples can be shared with a stranger of the same sex for 115 mk
per bed; Linnankatu 9, 00160 Helsinki, tel. 622-0470, fax 655
044). It's packed with facilities including a TV room, laundry
room, sauna, a members' kitchen with a refrigerator that lets you
lock up your caviar and beer, a cheap cafeteria, and plenty of
good budget information on travel to Russia or the Baltics.

Kallio Retkeilymaja is cozy, cheery, central, well run,
and very cheap (small—only 35 beds; 50 mk for dorm bed for

boys, or a bed in five-bed rooms for girls, sheets-10 mk;
lockers, kitchen facilities; closed 10:00–15:00, open
June–August; Porthaninkatu 2, tel. 7099 2590). From the
market square, take the metro or tram 3T, #1 or #2 to
Hakaniemi Square Market.

　　Olympic Stadium Hostel (Stadionin Retkeilymaja,
IYHF) is big, crowded, impersonal, and a last resort (54 mk
per bed with hostel membership in eight- to 12-bed rooms,
doubles-150 mk, sheets-15 mk, 15 mk extra per person with
no youth hostel card; open all year, dorm closed daily
10:00–16:00 off-season; tel. 496071). Take tram 7A to the
Olympic Stadium.

Transportation Connections—Helsinki

By Train
Helsinki to St. Petersburg and Moscow: Taking the train
from Helsinki is a speedy option, since Finland uses the wide
Russian track gauge and the wheels don't have to be changed.
Helsinki's train station is right downtown, within walking dis-
tance of most ferries. There are separate windows (#14–17) for
Russian and other international trains at the end of the
Helsinki train station ticket hall (Monday–Friday 8:30–17:00,
Saturday–Sunday 9:00–17:00). There are two trains a day to St.
Petersburg and one to Moscow. They take advance reserva-
tions at tel. 0100-128 (dialed in Finland) or 358/9/702-3411
(from elsewhere), fax 358/9/707-2111.

　　Going to St. Petersburg, the Finnish morning train is
much nicer than the Russian afternoon train. Going to

Trains Departing Helsinki

Destination	Leaves	Arrives	2nd class	1st class	Notes
St. Petersburg (Pietari)	6:30	13:41	265 mk	429 mk	Finnish *Sibelius*
St. Petersburg	15:32	23:13	265 mk	487 mk	Russian *Repin*
Moscow (Moskova)	17:08	8:56	504 mk	755 mk	Russian *Tolstoi*

Moscow, you'll save about 30 percent by taking the ferry to
Tallinn, and then the Tallinn–Moscow night train.

For train information, call 010-0121 (costs an initial 2 mk
plus 3.95 mk per minute).

By Bus
Helsinki to St. Petersburg: The Helsinki bus station is across
Mannerheimintie from the post office and train station. Bookings for all busses can be made at the station or by phone (tel.
6136-8433, fax 6136-8426).

Buses Departing Helsinki

Destination	Leaves	Arrives	Price	Students
St. Petersburg	7:15	16:05	207 mk	186 mk
St. Petersburg	9:00	17:50	220 mk	154 mk
St. Petersburg	12:00	20:15	230 mk	207 mk

By Boat
Baltic Line, which used to run ships between Helsinki and St.
Petersburg, has gone bankrupt, and it doesn't look like there
will be any cruises between Helsinki and St. Petersburg for at
least the next year or two.

Helsinki to Tallinn: During summer only, the fastest
way to Tallinn is by **hydrofoil**, which takes 1.5 to 2 hours. All
hydrofoils leave from the convenient Makasiiniterminaali,
within walking distance from the train station and the center of
Helsinki. Hydrofoil service starts sometime in April (depending on how fast the ice melts) and ends by November 1.
Schedules change a lot from year to year, but in mid-summer
there are as many as ten hydrofoil trips per day, fewer on Sundays. The first run leaves about 7:30 and the last about 18:00,
and it's just a matter of showing up at the Makasiiniterminaali
and waiting for the next boat (though on the most popular
departures you need to reserve a day or two in advance). Fares
range from 100 mk to 160 mk (no student discounts); the
cheaper fares are usually on evening departures from Helsinki
and morning departures from Tallinn.

Ferries run year-round between Helsinki and Tallinn and
normally take 3.5 to 4 hours. There are three to five runs a day,

leaving from the new Länsiterminaali in Helsinki's Western Harbor. This is convenient for drivers but requires foot passengers to use public transport: bus #15 from platform 46 at Helsinki's central bus station goes direct to Länsiterminaali every 15 to 30 minutes for 7 mk. Passenger tickets start at 90 mk, students 70 mk. In January and February, ice in the Gulf of Finland often slows or even stops ferry service.

You can reserve a ticket to Tallinn in four ways: by visiting any travel agency; by visiting the town offices of one of the shipping companies (open business hours only); by calling the companies' telephone reservations numbers (open a little longer) and then picking your ticket up at the port; or by going directly to the port (where ticket offices are open whenever ferries run). The ferry market between Helsinki and Tallinn is changeable, but names, office addresses, and telephone numbers of the main ferry operators in summer 1996 were: **Tallink** (Erottajankatu 19, hydrofoils tel. 358/9/2282-1277, ferries 2282-1211, fax 649-808); **Viking Line** (hydrofoils only, Mannerheimintie 14, tel. 12351, fax 647-075); **Eestin Linjat** (ferries only, Keskuskatu 1, tel. 228-8544, fax 2288-5222).

In 1996 all passenger ships sailing to Tallinn arrived at the main Tallinn Reisisadam ferry terminal, except for the Tallink hydrofoils which docked at the nearby Linnahall terminal. Both terminals are within walking distance of Tallinn's Old Town.

Helsinki to Stockholm: Silja and Viking lines sail between Helsinki and Stockholm daily, leaving about 18:00 and arriving about 9:00 the next morning. Ferry info in Helsinki: Viking Line, tel. 12351; Silja Line, tel. 9800-74552.

By Air
If you're 24 or under, Finnair youth fares are a good deal. A one-way flight to Tallinn costs $50, to Riga $125, and to Moscow $170. The Helsinki airport buses leave regularly from the Finnair City Terminal Building next to the train station.

STOCKHOLM
In this section, only transportation connections will be covered. For detailed information on Stockholm, consider *Rick Steves' Scandinavia 1997*.

Transportation Connections—Stockholm

By Boat

Stockholm to Tallinn: Estline's *Mare Balticum* and *Regina Balticum* connect Stockholm and Tallinn all year long. In summer 1996 for the first time there were two ferries and daily service in both directions, and this will probably be true in summer 1997 although off-season they may cut back to one ferry with service every other day. Stockholm departures are at 17:30, arriving in Tallinn at 9:00 the next morning; Tallinn departures are at 19:00, arriving in Stockholm at 9:00 (all times local; Stockholm is an hour earlier than Tallinn). Ticket prices are changing but start at about U.S. $45 for one-way deck passage (students with an ISIC card get about 25 percent off, and there's also a round-trip discount). Cabins start at about $10 for a berth in a four-person room beneath the waterline. Fares are about 20 percent higher for Friday and Saturday departures. In Stockholm, reserve by calling 08/667-0001 (you can pick up the tickets at the port). Bus #41 runs between the Frihamnen harbor in Stockholm, where the ferry docks, and the center of town (13 Swedish kronor).

You can also take an overnight ferry from Stockholm to Helsinki, then another ferry or hydrofoil from Helsinki to Tallinn. You can take either Silja Line or Viking Line from Stockholm to Helsinki, but the Silja Line terminal is right next to the Tallinn hydrofoil terminal in Helsinki. Although this route takes longer, the ships are a little more luxurious and you get to see Helsinki too. Another advantage of this approach is that railpass holders get a free or discounted trip to Helsinki.

Stockholm to St. Petersburg: Baltic Line, which used to run ships on this route, has gone bankrupt.

By Air

Stockholm to Tallinn and Riga: If you're 24 or under, SAS youth fares to Tallinn and Riga are a good deal (reservable up to seven days in advance). SAS has one-way youth fares from Stockholm to Tallinn and Riga for $151 and $158 respectively. Estonian Air has comparable youth fares on its daily flights to Tallinn.

WARSAW

For detailed information on Warsaw, consider *Poland*, published by Lonely Planet. Canadians need a visa for Poland (the consulate in Toronto is at 416/252-5471). Americans just need their passports.

Transportation Connections—Warsaw

Trains: International train tickets are available from the international ticket windows (Kasy Międzynarodowe) on the top floor of Warsaw's Warszawa Centralna train station. Usually at least one of the agents on duty speaks English.

Crossing the border by train: Finland, the Baltics, and Russia use the Russian railroad gauge, which is wider than that used in Poland and the rest of Europe. Since trains have to change gauges at the border, passengers either wait while new bogies (wheel assemblies) are put on their car, or move into new cars with correctly-spaced wheels.

Buses: Most buses out of Warsaw leave from the Warszawa Zachodnia bus station. To reach it, take bus #127 west along al. Jerozolimskie from just outside the Warszawa Centralna train station, and get off at the last stop. Buy tickets at the "Kasa Międzynarodowa" window on the south end of the waiting hall.

By Bus

Warsaw to Vilnius: It's easiest by bus. In summer 1996 there were four buses a day: two day-runs leaving at 8:30 and 11:00, and two overnights at 18:30 and 19:30. Fares were $14–$16. All the buses left from the main Warszawa Zachodnia station except the 11:00, which used Warszawa Wschodnia station. The trip to Vilnius takes about ten hours.

By Train

Warsaw to Vilnius: If you must go by train to Vilnius, the best option is to travel to Kaunas (see below), spend the night, then continue to Vilnius (another two hours) in the morning. There *is* a direct Warsaw–Vilnius night train, but since it crosses through Grodno in Belarus, you get woken up in the middle of the night four times by customs officers and once by bogie-changing, plus you need a Belarussian transit visa— hassles you can do without.

Warsaw to Kaunas, Riga, and Tallinn: The Baltic Express (the Warsaw–Tallinn train) leaves Warsaw at 14:42 daily, arriving in Kaunas at 23:52, Riga at 5:00 the next day, and Tallinn at 11:55. At 22:00, just after crossing the border

Between Poland and Lithuania by Rail

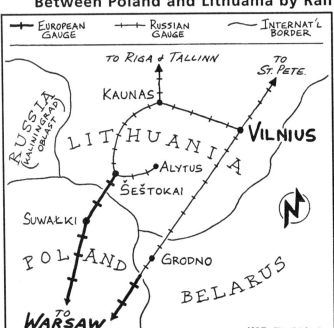

into Lithuania, you have to move into new carriages (which use the wider Russian railway gauge) at the Šeštokai station. Warsaw–Tallinn tickets cost about $51 for second class, $82 for first class.

There's also direct daily overnight bus service from Warsaw to Riga for about $20.

Warsaw to Moscow: The *Polonez* train leaves Warsaw every afternoon at 14:52 and arrives in Moscow the following day at 12:19. A second-class (three-bed) sleeping berth costs $68; a first-class (two-bed) berth costs $110. Your Russian visa will be valid for transit across Belarus. Several other trains make the run from Warsaw to Moscow on their way from Berlin, Prague, and the like, but since the Polonez originates in Warsaw, the cars will be cleaner and the conductors less sleepy when you board.

Warsaw to St. Petersburg: While there's a daily train from Warsaw to St. Petersburg (the distance and cost are almost the same as to Moscow), these trains pass through

Belarus, Lithuania, and Latvia on the way. According to the Belarussian consulate in New York (summer 1996), if you have a valid Russian visa it will be accepted for transit across Belarus on this train, but do confirm this before you go (see below). Frankly, because of all the border checks it makes more sense to fly from Warsaw to St. Petersburg, or to go by train via Moscow.

Belarussian Visas: If you simply *must* take one of the direct trains between Warsaw and Vilnius, it is possible to get a Belarussian transit visa from the consulate in Warsaw (Atenska ul. 67, tel. 617-3212) or in Vilnius (Muitines gatvė 41, tel. 230 626) for about $30 (same or next day processing). You need to show them your ticket. We've heard that it's still possible to get the transit visa at the border, for $45 plus a lot of annoyance. Since the very existence of Belarus as a separate country is in doubt given their recent union agreement with Russia, if you are planning to cross Belarus we suggest you confirm the regulations with the Belarussian embassy (1619 New Hampshire Ave. NW, Washington, DC 20009, tel. 202/986-1604, or the consulate at 708 3rd Ave., 21st floor, New York, NY 10017, tel. 212/682-5392).

By Air

If you're flying out of Warsaw, the Polish airline LOT has some excellent deals for all ages. For example: $146 round-trip to Vilnius, $175 to Riga, $261 to St. Petersburg, and $285 to Moscow. The LOT ticket office is on the ground floor of the Marriott Hotel in Warsaw. In the U.S., call LOT at 800/223-0593.

RUSSIA

MOSCOW

Moscow encapsulates all that's good and all that's bad about Russia. Like the country, its vast size threatens to overwhelm you and swallow you up. You feel small under the press of its weighty buildings, starchy food, grime, and pollution. Among the sprawling tenement buildings and "Stalin Gothic" skyscrapers one can still find brilliant golden domes and reminders of Czarist days. But the Soviet penchant for gigantism forces the visitor to search out these glimpses of Russia's past like flowers in a field of tall grass.

Moscow lacks the inherent beauty of St. Petersburg, but visitors here will feel as though they are in a place where things are happening furiously. Some days Moscow will leave you mentally and physically exhausted, wondering why you decided to go there and when the plane is leaving. Other days, though, you almost like it.

The city is huge. Rides around the center can take an hour. And the contradictions that pervade its society take you on an emotional roller coaster. Russians will bump, shove, and yell at you in a bakery line, and then smile and offer you everything they have in their kitchen when you dine at their apartments. The cramped and crumbling apartments constructed by Brezhnev are so unattractive that even the simplest church seems incredibly beautiful. Moscow's nouveau riche streak around in their mud-splattered Mercedes and BMWs, while young mothers stand alongside *babushki* selling everything from dried fish to a used pair of boots. For many Russians life is a game of survival, and during these times of awkward steps towards a market economy, the rules seem to change every day.

Russophiles are evenly split between those who prefer Moscow and those who would choose nowhere else but St. Petersburg. Regardless of how or whether it charms you, Moscow is an exciting city to visit.

Planning Your Time
Plan on at least two days in Moscow. For a good visit, try this schedule:

Day 1
10:00 Arrive in Red Square by Metro, see St. Basil's, visit Lenin, and wander through the GUM department store.
13:00 Grab a quick lunch inside GUM, or at Kombi's or McDonald's on Tverskaya.
14:00 Depending on the weather and your interests, head to the Izmailovskii Park flea market, the Tretyakov Gallery, Novodevichi cemetery and convent, or "any random metro neighborhood" (explained under Sights, below).
18:00 Return to the center for dinner at Patio Pizza.

Day 2
10:00 Tour the Kremlin.
11:30 Walk along Volkhonka past the Pushkin Museum and the Church of Christ the Savior, then cut up along the Boulevard Ring to the Arbat. Break for lunch at Patio Pizza or at the Georgian restaurant on the Arbat.
15:00 Stroll down the Arbat and then return to the center along the almost-parallel Novii Arbat.
18:00 Walk or take the subway up ulitsa Tverskaya to Mayakovskaya Metro station for dinner at one of the nearby restaurants.

Orientation
Moscow is enormous and daunting to the uninitiated. The city is organized in concentric circles. The outer ring road marks the city limits while most of the important sights are contained within the inner Garden Ring or the innermost Boulevard Ring. At the bull's-eye are the Kremlin and Red Square. The Moscow River cuts an arc through the center of the city, with its peak touching the Kremlin.

Tourist Information: There's no central tourist office. One

Moscow

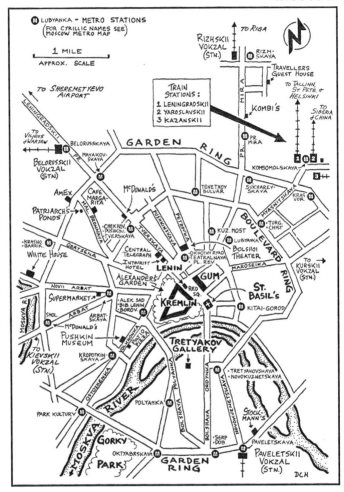

way to get acquainted with the city is on one of Intourist's efficient, reasonably priced, half-day tours which leave daily at 14:30 from the tall Hotel Intourist on Tverskaya, near the Kremlin ($10). If your tour includes Moscow University, you'll get a great panoramic view of the city.

American Embassy: Novinskii/НОВИНСКИЙ bulvar 19/23, tel. 252-2451. Metro: Barrikadnaya/Ђаррикадная.

News: The excellent English-language *Moscow Times*,

which comes out Tuesday through Saturday, will keep you up-to-date on events in the capital and elsewhere in Russia. It's free at many stores, restaurants, and hotels.

Bookstores: The most convenient is **Zwemmers,** which has a modest stock of art books and fiction shipped in from England (Monday–Saturday 10:00–19:00, Kuznetskii Most/Куэнецкий Мост Most 18, near the Kuznetskii Most Metro station). Less accessibly, a few tiny one-room bookstores have opened around 1st Novokuznetskaya pereulok 5, between Paveletskaya and Novokuznetskaya Metro stations.

Currency Exchange
5,000 rubles = about $1
Every neighborhood, often every block, sometimes every store has its own Обмен Валюты (currency exchange) desk, usually run by a bank. Little offices—even the exchange shacks inside shops—give better rates than desks in major hotels. A sizable number of banks now change traveler's checks, but it is still better to bring cash. A commission of 3 percent on traveler's checks is a good deal here. ATMs have arrived—there's one in the Novoarbatskii Gastronom on the Novii Arbat (see under Grocery Stores below).

The Moscow branch of American Express is a little out of the way and you should try to do your banking elsewhere, but it does provide the usual menu of services. If you lose your card or checks and have to go to American Express, exit the Mayakovskaya/Маяковская Metro station and cross the street to the tower with the blue clock on it; then walk about 3 blocks along the Ring (Monday–Friday 9:00–17:00, Saturday 9:00–13:00, ulitsa Sadovaya-Kudrinskaya/Садовая-Кудринская 21a, tel. 956-9019).

Telephones and Mail
For local calls you can use almost any public pay phone (there's no difference between a Таксофон and a Телефон). They have been converted to take small brown plastic tokens sold at Metro entrances for 25 cents. Many pay phones are out of order. Lift the receiver, listen for the dial tone, dial, and wait for an answer or at least until it starts ringing before you put in your token.

You can do it all from mailing a postcard to placing a call at the Central Telegraph Office (ulitsa Tverskaya/Тверская 7,

Metro: Okhotnii Ryad/Охотный Ряд). For long-distance calls
within the former U.S.S.R., go to the little room to the left in
the vestibule (daily 7:00–22:00). Pay first, then you can call.
Rates have risen dramatically (60 cents/minute to St. Petersburg). You can also use a private phone or go to any local post
office.

The post office hall is on the right as you enter the
Central Telegraph Office (windows open Monday–Friday
8:00–21:00, Saturday 8:00–19:00, Sunday 9:00–19:00, lunch
break daily 14:00–15:00). If you want to send a postcard, go to
the window in the back left corner of the hall to buy stamps,
then put your card in one of the boxes in the vestibule. It will
take anywhere from a week to two months. If you actually want
to communicate with someone, a better bet for value and speed
is Global Sprint Fax. Go to window #13 on the left-hand side.
You leave your document; they scan it and it's computer-sent;
they notify you by phone if it fails to go through. One page to
the U.S. or Western Europe costs about $2.50.

Getting Around Moscow

Get used to the Metro. The stops (identifiable by a glowing
red M) are never much more than a ten-minute walk away
inside the Garden Ring road. If you do not see one, just ask
any passerby "Gdye stantsiya Metro?" (or show them this: Где
станция метро?) and you will likely be answered by *"Vot"* and
an outstretched arm pointing the way.

Tokens for the Metro (currently 30 cents apiece) are available from windows inside each station entrance. The latest
price should be posted near the ticket window. Go to the window, hold up the requisite number of fingers and say the number of tokens you want. For trams and buses you need to buy
tickets which the drivers sell in strips of ten. They're also sold
in and around Metro ticket windows.

Sights—Central Moscow

Essential sightseeing in Moscow means the very center—the
Kremlin and Red Square—plus three streets that radiate from
it: Volkhonka, the Arbat, and Tverskaya.

▲▲▲**Red Square**—Any tour of Moscow should begin on Red
Square in front of St. Basil's Cathedral. Surrounded on one
side by the Kremlin walls and Lenin's Mausoleum and on the
other by GUM, the largest department store in the country,

Moscow Metro

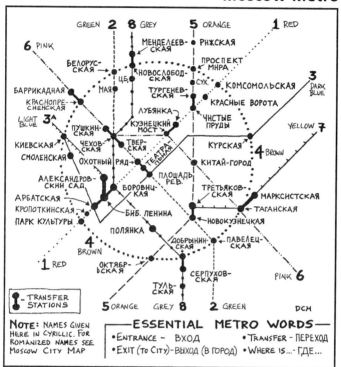

you'll rightly feel at the administrative heart of a grand empire.

▲▲**Lenin's Mausoleum**—Though there is no longer any ceremonial changing of the guard in front of the mausoleum, you can go inside for free and decide for yourself whether Lenin is wax or flesh (Tuesday, Wednesday, Thursday, Saturday, and Sunday from 10:00–13:00). Large bags and cameras must be checked in the cloakroom on the side of the maroon-colored, closed Historical Museum.

▲**St. Basil's Cathedral**—Red Square's top ornament is St. Basil's Cathedral. Now more of a plain museum with some old icons and a barren maze of rooms than a living church, its exterior is far more interesting than its interior. Even so, after you've given the outside a 360-degree marvel, consider peeking inside.

▲▲**GUM (ГУМ)**—This is the best-stocked department store in Russia. Since 1992, hard-currency stores such as Benetton,

Central Moscow

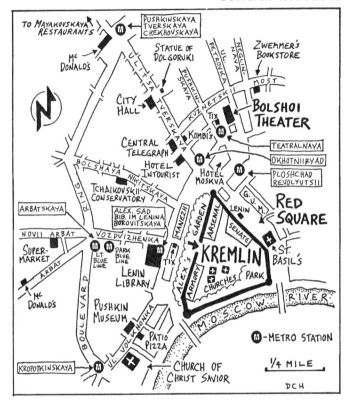

Galeries Lafayette, and Samsonite have slowly begun to take over more and more space in GUM. There are three corridors; enter at either end. Climb up to the top floor at either end of the building where there are no stores and treat yourself to a spectacular view and an amazing vantage point for photographing ordinary Russians as they go about their shopping unawares. The natural light from the skylights is especially pretty on bright days. There's a fast-food chicken restaurant and a stand-up pizza joint inside. (Monday–Saturday 8:00–20:00.)

▲▲▲The Kremlin—A must-see, the Kremlin is a walled enclosure containing Russia's top government offices, as well as several beautiful Orthodox churches. The entrance is through Alexandrovskii Sad (Alexander's Garden); from Red Square, walk north past the mausoleum out of the square, go left into the garden and past the Tomb of the Unknown Soldier, and you'll come to the white Kremlin entrance tower, across from the Alexandrovskii Sad/Александровский Сад Metro exit. Ticket booths are beside the tower. You have to check your bags at the little office under the stairs.

The Kremlin is open Friday through Wednesday from 10:00–17:00 (ticket office closes from 13:00–14:00 and at 16:30; closed Thursdays and during frequent official functions). Entry to the Kremlin grounds costs only 20 cents, and lets you walk around the grounds, scan the Moscow River from the park along the south wall, pat the huge cannon and broken bell, and admire the church-domes, towers, and congress buildings. For foreigners, entrance to the four churches costs $6 per church, students half-price. You don't have to see all four churches, and you can pay at the church door after you've peered inside and decided. Getting into the Armory costs $14, students half price.

On summer mornings, watch for newlywed brides and grooms who come to lay flowers at the Tomb of the Unknown Soldier back in Alexandrovskii Sad.

▲▲**The Arbat** (Арбат)—Once a prestigious address for Russia's eminent writers, this pedestrian street not only retains some of its original grandeur but also has the city's best concentration of kitschy tourist shops and (in summer) outdoor cafés. McDonald's graces its far end.

You can walk to the Arbat from the Kremlin entrance, going past the Lenin Library down ulitsa Vozdvizhenka/ Воздвиженка, or along the Boulevard Ring from Kropotkinskaya Metro and the Church of Christ the Savior. The closest Metro is the Arbatskaya/Арбатская station on the light blue line, directly across from the beginning of the Arbat—go through the underground passage full of middle-aged women selling puppies and kittens while artists offer to sketch you. The Arbatskaya station on the dark blue line is also convenient: exit, turn left, and walk through the crowds for about 250 meters. The Smolenskaya/Смоленская station on the dark blue line is at the Arbat's outer end.

The **Novii Arbat,** just north of and nearly parallel to the Arbat, was built in the 1960s, and the huge apartment buildings that line it like so many open books were intended as a showpiece of Soviet success. It's now one of Moscow's most important modern shopping streets. If you want to see the **White**

House (Белый Дом), the scene of the October 1993 shelling
which finished the standoff between Boris Yeltsin and his hard-
line foes in the Russian parliament, you can continue all the
way down the Novii Arbat to the river (taking the Metro to
Krasnopresnenskaya/Краснопресненская on the Ring line or
Smolenskaya/Смоленская on the light blue line will get you
part of the way).

▲**Pushkin Museum** (Музей им. Пушкина)—The museum is
less remarkable for its standing collections (roomfuls of paintings by Monet, Renoir, van Gogh, Rembrandt, and Picasso)
than for its temporary shows—in 1996, these included the
Trojan Gold and the "Moscow-Berlin 1900–1950" exhibit of
totalitarian art (Tuesday–Sunday 10:00–19:00, admission until
18:00, $6, students $3). The Pushkin Museum and Church of
Christ the Savior (below) are within a couple blocks of each
other (and Red Square) on Ulitsa Volkhonka/Волхонка, which
runs away from the Kremlin from the southern end of Alexandrovskii Sad and the southwest corner of the Kremlin itself.

▲▲**Church of Christ the Savior** (Храм Христа Спасителя)—
Originally built here in the 19th century, the church was torn
down under Stalin, and a monstrous Palace of Soviets with a
towering statue of Lenin was planned. When the ground
proved too soft, the site was turned into a public swimming
pool, demolished in 1994–95. Until the church opens (sometime in 1997), a temporary exhibit allows you to watch its
reconstruction, see plans and a scale model, and learn about
the history of the site (free, daily 10:00–18:00). Across the
street is the Boulevard Ring—along which it's a 10- to 15-
minute walk to the Arbat—and the Kropotkinskaya/
Кропоткинская Metro station.

▲▲**Ulitsa Tverskaya** (Тверская)—This is Moscow's most
prestigious street. Don't miss the walk south down Tverskaya
from Mayakovskaya or Pushkinskaya Metro stops to the Kremlin. You'll pass the Tchaikovskii concert hall, the original
Moscow McDonald's and many more upscale restaurants, the
city hall and mounted statue of Yuri Dolgoruki (founder of
Moscow), the Central Telegraph Office, the Intourist Hotel,
and finally the National Hotel at the corner across from the
Kremlin.

▲▲**Classical Music or Ballet**—Scout out posters and ask at
your hotel or hostel for advice on music, opera, and ballet performances. In contrast to the cleaned-up situation in St.

Petersburg, getting into the Bolshoi Ballet still usually requires paying scalpers these days (the going rate is about $10), but you can try at the ticket office across the square from the theater, next to the Teatralnaya/Театральная Metro entrance, between 12:00 and 18:00. Opera and ballet in the Palace of Congresses, inside the Kremlin, is also an option; tickets are cheaper and scalpers usually don't bother with them. The ticket office (open 12:00–14:00 and 15:00–19:00) is kitty-corner from the Kremlin entrance, to the left if you stand with your back to the tower.

It's always possible to hear great classical concerts for pennies at the Tchaikovskii Concert Hall at Metro: Mayakovskaya/Маяковская, or in the two halls of the Tchaikovskii Conservatory about 3 blocks along Bolshaya Nikitskaya ulitsa from the Kremlin (on the left). Look in the *Moscow Times* for listings and stop by for tickets a day or so in advance. Most concerts and performances start at 19:00.

Sights—Outer Moscow

▲▲**Izmailovskii Park weekend flea market**—This is the place to buy your souvenirs. Most often you are dealing with the original artists, and bargaining is a must. Pick up a 13-piece *matryoshka* doll, beautifully hand-carved chess sets, or scarves and patchwork quilts. To get to the market, take the dark blue Metro line four stops northeast of the Ring line to Izmailovskii Park/Измайловский Парк—it's the station with a third track in the middle. Exit, turn left, and walk past the huge hotel toward the stadium and smokestacks in the distance. Notice the Intourist propaganda posters on the right along the way. (Open only on weekends and holidays, from morning till evening.)

▲**The All-Russian Exhibition Center** (VDNKh/ВДНХ)—Once the Exhibit of the People's Economic Achievements, this center was a temple to the proletariat. Built in the 1930s, its 72 Neoclassical pavilions glorify Pig Husbandry, Standardization, Atomic Energy, and other giddy arts. Today it's hard to believe VDNKh was ever anything but a mall waiting to happen. Electronics is the name of the game, and every single structure has been transformed into a rabbit-hutch of cut-rate consumerism. Fascinating. VDNKh is located on Prospekt Mira opposite the Kosmos Hotel (concessions open 10:00–17:00, near Metro: VDNKh/ВДНХ).

▲▲**Any random Metro station**—To get a real feel for Russian life, try taking the Metro to any of the stations outside Moscow's Ring line. You can pick one at random, but here are some recommendations. For true Soviet residential bleakness it is hard to beat Yasenevo/Ясенево or Konkovo/Коньково, south on the orange line. If you prefer your bleakness dirty and industrial, head to the southeast, Moscow's most polluted region: Volgogradskii Prospekt/Волгоградский Проспект and Tekstilshchiki/Текстильщики on the pink line. A more desirable neighborhood surrounds the Krylatskoe/Крылатское station at the end of the light blue line in the west of Moscow. Here the prevailing west winds are still unpolluted by the city's factories, and the 18-story tower blocks were built only recently. In another well-regarded neighborhood, around Sokol/Сокол to the north on the green line, you can see Stalin-era buildings from the forties and fifties. In each case, check out the stores that Russians shop in as they walk from the Metro exit to their apartments after work each day.

Enjoy the Metro on your way. The most beautiful station is Mayakovskaya/Маяковская on the green line (don't miss the ceiling mosaics). Ploshchad Revolyutsii/Площадь Революции has arresting socialist-realist statues. The grandest stations are on the Ring line and the dark blue line.

▲**Novodevichi Cemetery** (Новодевичье Кладбище) **and Convent**—The walled convent, with its churches and graves, is one of the most peaceful places to escape to on a nice day in Moscow. Entrance to the grounds is usually free; if you want to see the museums inside you'll pay $5 (Wednesday–Monday 10:00–17:00, closed Tuesday). The cemetery, adjacent to the convent but with a separate entrance, contains the graves of Chekhov, Gogol, Bulgakov, Mayakovsky, Eisenstein, Shostakovich, Scriabin, Khrushchev, Molotov, Gromyko, and Stalin's wife, among others. It's one of the few major attractions in Moscow without a separate price for foreigners: entrance costs $2 for everyone (daily 10:00–18:00). Ask them for their English map ($2). To reach the complex, take the red line Metro two stops southeast of the Ring to Sportivnaya/Спортивная, go out the exit towards the center, turn right and walk about 4 blocks along ulitsa 10-letiya Oktyabrya, and you'll see the spires of the convent across the street to your left. The cemetery is past the convent to your left.

▲**Gorky Park** (Парк Горкого)—Perhaps the best reason to
go is the view from atop the enormous rickety Ferris wheel
in the center of the 300-acre park (daily 10:00–22:30). To get
to the park, take the Metro to the Oktyabrskaya/Октябрь-
ская Ring line station, exit to the street through the right-
hand doors, go left around the corner, and walk alongside the
park's fence about 400 meters to the huge colonnaded
entrance. Tickets are sold at the windows to the left and
right for a few cents. Consider going back downtown on a
riverboat, which you can catch at the terminal on the river
side of the park.

▲**Tretyakov Gallery**—To get to the Tretyakov Gallery,
which has the world's best collection of Russian icons and a
selection of 18th- and 19th-century art (especially portraiture),
take the orange line Metro to Tretyakovskaya/Третьяковская
(don't go out through the connected Novokuznetskaya station,
which will leave you several blocks away). Turn left at the top
of the stairs, cross the street, and walk down the brick road
about 100 meters to the large red and white building on the
right ($6, students half price, Tuesday–Sunday 10:00–20:00,
ticket windows close at 19:00, closed Monday).

▲**Sergiev Posad** (Сергиев Посад)—Formerly called Zagorsk,
this is a living medieval monastery 60 km outside of Moscow
(Tuesday–Sunday 10:00–18:00, closed Monday). This world of
onion domes and icons, one of the most beautiful churches in all
Russia, is 90 minutes by local train from Moscow's Yaroslavskii
Station (Metro: Komsomolskaya/Комсомольская). Coming out
of the Metro, go in the glassed-in building under the large
MOCKBA sign and buy an eight-zone *obratny* (return) ticket
from any of the ticket windows (about $3), then hop on any of
the trains marked Sergiev Posad or Aleksandrov (Александров),
which leave every 10–30 minutes.

Sleeping in Moscow
(If calling from the U.S., dial 011-7-095, then the local num-
ber; for more phone info, see the Appendix: Direct Dialing
Within the Baltics & Russia.)

Overall, here's our recommendation for Moscow: If you
have friends or relatives there, stay with them even if it
means buying your visa support letter from IRO Travel at
the Traveller's Guest House, or from wherever you plan to
stay in St. Petersburg. If you're willing to pay $200 a night

for a double, go to your nearest travel agent and reserve a room at one of the fancy hotels. If neither of these is an option, consider going on a group tour or buying a flight-plus-hotel package. If you're a dyed-in-the-wool budget traveler who can't live without a cheap bed, try the following, though we must admit that the thought of staying at any of these places doesn't fill our hearts with joy:

The **Travellers Guest House** has been Moscow's main youth hostel for the past few years, although it's not as clean or well-run as the St. Petersburg hostel. It occupies two floors of a typical Soviet student dormitory, in which every two rooms share an entranceway and bathroom. A bed in a four-bed room costs $18, while a double costs $45 and a single goes for $35. The hot water goes off for a few weeks every summer. The clientele is heavily American and British. Reserve early (Bolshaya Pereyaslavskaya/Большая Переяславская ulitsa 50, tenth floor, tel. 971-4059, fax 280-7686, E-mail tgh@glas.apc.org). It's about a 15-minute walk from Metro: Prospekt Mira/Проспект мира, walk north about 3 blocks, turn right along the street with the four smokestacks in the distance, walk 1 block to the end of the street, turn left, and the guest house is in the tall white building on your right with red signs on either side of the door. Go in and take the elevator up to the tenth floor.

The Travellers Guest House also has an in-house travel agency called **IRO Travel** (tel. 974-1781 or 974-1798, fax 280-7686, E-mail iro@glas.apc.org) which can help with plane and train tickets, and can also fax you visa support documentation—in other words, the invitation letter which you submit to the consulate to get your visa—regardless of whether or not you plan to stay at TGH. When you arrive in Moscow and come to their office, they will register you while you wait. The cheapest invitation, for a one-month tourist visa, costs $35. A one-year multi-entry visa invitation costs $320. Contact them from anywhere in the world by fax or E-mail with your full name, citizenship, passport number, birthdate, and city where you plan to apply for the visa. They normally ask for prepayment by credit card.

Heritage Hostel is a new youth hostel in Moscow. You can contact them directly or book through the St. Petersburg International Hostel (Kosmonavtov/Космонавтов ulitsa 2, tel. 975-3501, E-mail evgen@az-tour.msk.ru).

For homestay possibilities, contact **White Nights** (in USA, tel./fax 314/991-5512) or the **Russia Experience** (in USA, tel. 800/683-7403, fax 508/792-0065).

Eating in Moscow

The first thing that should be said about restaurants in Moscow is that you will find few average locals at them, as the prices are prohibitive to all but the wealthiest. Most Muscovites dine outside their homes only at weddings. Even for Americans Moscow restaurant prices are extremely high because of the expense-account Western consultant clientele.

McDonald's (МакДоналдс) golden arches attract Muscovites and foreigners alike with cleanliness, efficiency, relatively cheap prices, and predictably edible food. Indeed, this is the place to go when a quick lunch must be squeezed into a full day's sightseeing or when dinner plans fall through. Moscow's oldest and biggest McDonald's is at Metro: Pushkinskaya/ Пушкинская, directly across from the statue of Russia's beloved national poet, Aleksandr Pushkin. In the best tradition of Soviet gigantism and American capitalism, Mickey D's boasts 27 cash registers, 1,500 employees with beaming smiles, seating for over 700, and nearly 40,000 customers a day. It even has its own farm to ensure an adequate supply of all the sesame seeds and special sauce required to make the Big Mac you try here taste like the one you last ate back in the States. There are sometimes lines, but they move fast. There are now six other McDonald's in Moscow. Another big one is at the outer end of the Arbat, behind Metro: Smolenskaya/ Смоленская. It is sometimes less crowded, and the upstairs room is a nicer place to sit and linger. A third, small McDonald's, with limited seating, is across from Central Telegraph on Gazetnii/Газетный pereulok, a side street just off Tverskaya, near Metro: Okhotnii Ryad/Охотный Ряд. A fourth is at Metro: Prospekt Mira/Проспект Мира. At each location, a Big Mac, large Coke, and large fries cost about $4.25 total (daily 8:00–24:00).

Kombi's (Комби'с) is Moscow's closest thing to a Western sub shop, selling sandwiches for $3–$5 and their trademark Oreo milkshakes for $1.75. They have an English menu. There are several locations in Moscow, all open daily from 10:00 to 22:00. One is very near Red Square at ulitsa Tverskaya/ Тверская 4, across the street from the Hotel Intourist near

Metro: Okhotnii Ryad/Охотный Ряд; another is at ulitsa Tverskaya 32, across the street from the exit of Metro: Mayakovskaya/Маяковская (go left at the top of the escalators); another is at Arbat 40. A fourth Kombi's is at Metro: Prospekt Mira/Проспект Мира; go out the Ring line exit so you don't have to cross the street, then walk a block up to Prospekt Mira 48. This is extremely convenient for people staying at the Travellers Guest House.

If you have never tried **Georgian cuisine**, Moscow is a good place to do it. It's an easy choice especially for vegetarians. The most convenient Georgian restaurant in Moscow is the **Restoran Mziuri** in the basement of the Georgian Cultural Center at Arbat 42 (daily 12:00–24:00). More popular is **Guria** (Гурия), at Komsomolskii/Комсомольский prospekt 7/3, in the courtyard near the corner of ulitsa Timura Frunze (Metro: Park Kultury/Парк Културы). In both cases it is advisable to go only for lunch when reservations are unnecessary. At neither should a full meal cost you more than $12.

The secret to ordering Georgian food is appetizers. A nice Georgian meal for three or four might consist of one each of the following: *khachapuri* (хачапури—dough filled with cheese), a chopped vegetable dish such as *pkhali* (пхали—chopped cabbage), chicken *satsivi* (сациви—diced chicken in a spicy yellow sauce), *baklazhan* (баклажан—eggplant), *lobio* (Лобио—a bean dish served either hot or cold), and plenty of *lavash* (лаваш— bread). If you want soup, try *kharcho* (харчо), a spicy broth with lots of meat and onions. Main dishes are less special, usually just some kind of grilled or skewered meat. Tell them you don't eat meat, order two or three appetizers per person, and you'll cut down the size of the bill and still get the best dishes.

Patio Pizza (Патио Пицца) is a large pizza, pasta, and salad restaurant with trademark red- and-white checked tablecloths and glassed-in terraces. It seems more a part of American suburbia than of Moscow. A good all-you-can-eat salad bar costs $8, whole pizzas start at $7, lasagna or tortellini is $11, and credit cards are accepted. One location is at ulitsa Volkhonka/Волхонка 13a, across the street from the Pushkin Museum; you can walk from the Kremlin, or take the Metro to Kropotkinskaya/Кропоткинская (go out the exit towards the center). The other Patio Pizza is in the terrace underneath the Hotel Intourist on ulitsa Tverskaya/Тверская. (Both open daily 12:00–24:00.)

Near the **Mayakovskaya**/Маяковская Metro station at the top end of ulitsa Tverskaya/Тверская is a potpourri of good restaurants. **Patio Pasta**, related to Patio Pizza, is on the northwest corner of the square (1st Tverskaya-Yam-skaya/1я Тверская-Ямская ulitsa 1, open daily 12:00–24:00, pasta dishes $7–$12). On the southeast corner of the square at ulitsa Tverskaya 30 is **Tandoor**, an Indian restaurant with vegetable entrees for $8–$11 and meat entrees for $14–$19 (order rice separately for $3; daily 12:00–23:00). Across the street at ulitsa Tverskaya 32 is the **American Bar & Grill** (Американский Бар & Гриль), with salads and burgers from $6, and burritos for $10, as well as breakfast (open 24 hours), and next door are the purple columns of **Kombi's** (see above). For Kombi's, the American Bar & Grill, and Tandoor, go left at the top of the escalators if you're coming from the Metro.

Inside **GUM** are a few quick stand-up and fast-food restaurants, not worth a special trip but fine for signtseers who need a midday sandwich. For example **Rostik's** (Ростик'с), on the second floor of GUM in the northeast corner, is a fast-food chicken restaurant where it costs $3.50 to gnaw on two pieces of roast chicken and a roll (daily 10:00–20:00; use the separate entrance on Sunday).

Farmer's market: Central Moscow's largest and best market is the Danilovskii Rynok (Даниловский Рынок). Take the Metro one stop south of the Ring on the gray line to Tulskaya/Тульская. Exit toward the center and make your way across the busy intersection to the large circular building with the white, dome-like top.

Grocery stores: These are proliferating in Moscow, and it is no longer necessary to trek halfway across the city to find a decent selection of groceries. One of the best supermarkets in Moscow—although it still uses the three-line system—is the **Novoarbatskii Gastronom** at Novii Arbat/Новыи Арбат 21. From Metro: Arbatskaya/Арбатская, walk about three minutes down Novii Arbat, the street with the monstrous gray Soviet architecture that radiates from the same point as the Arbat pedestrian zone. It's on your left. The downstairs section has a particularly good selection of quality Russian products. Upstairs is a separate open-shelf section with imported goods only (Monday–Saturday 9:00–22:00, Sunday 10:00–20:00).

Station Guide

Trains to:	Leave from:	Nearest Metro:
Warsaw and Vilnius	Belorusskii Vokzal	Belorusskaya/ Белорусская
Riga	Rizhskii Vokzal	Rizhskaya/Рижская
Tallinn and St. Petersburg	Leningradskii Vokzal	Komsomolskaya/ Комсомольская

Transportation Connections—Moscow

By Train

Foreigners in Moscow normally buy train tickets at one of the four offices of the Moscow Central Railway Agency. You can visit whichever office is most convenient; I prefer the Krasno-prudnaya ulitsa office at Metro: Komsomolskaya. The following offices are open daily 8:00–13:00 and 14:00–19:00.

Moscow's Railway Offices

Krasnoprudnaya/Краснопрудная ulitsa 1, on the first floor of the brown 9-floor apartment building next to Yaroslavskii Vokzal at Metro: Komsomolskaya/Комсомольская. It says Центральное Железнодорожное Агенство in green letters over the door. Windows 10–11 are for foreigners buying tickets to destinations within the ex–Soviet Union. Windows 4–7 are for tickets to foreign countries like Poland and Finland. Window 3 is for information, and window 2 is the *administrator* (the office boss).

Leningradskii/Ленинградский prospekt 1, behind Belorusskii Vokzal (station). Metro: Belorusskaya/ Белорусская. You can reach it by crossing the bridge across the tracks to the yellow and white building; go in the farthest entrance.

Mozhaiskii/Можайский Val 4/6, near Metro: Kievskaya/ Киевская.

Malii Kharitonevskii/Малый Харитоньевский pereulok 6/11 (the head office, but the least convenient). From Metro: Turgenevskaya/Тургеневская, walk northeast on ulitsa Myas-nitskaya/Мясницкая; take second right onto Griboyedova.

Foreigners are usually not permitted to buy tickets from the

Trains Departing Moscow

#	To	Leaves	Arrives	2nd class	1st class
1	Riga (Рига)	19:14	10:50	$42	$80
3	"	20:53	12:15	"	"
34	Tallinn (Таллинн)	17:25	9:04	$41	$79
5	Vilnius (Вильнюс)	17:17	7:56	$38	$72
9	Warsaw (Варшава)	15:25	9:13	$68	$110
32	Helsinki (Хельсинки)	8:30	9:02	$93	$136
24	St. Petersburg				
	(Санкт-Петербург)	12:27	20:50	$39	$65
160	"	17:20	23:09	"	"
14	"	20:35	4:50	"	"
28	"	21:44	5:45	"	"
10	"	22:50	6:40	"	"
26	"	23:00	7:10	"	"
6	"	23:10	7:38	"	"
2	"	23:55	8:25	"	"
4		23:59	8:29	$38	$73
12	"	0:45	8:50	"	"
20	"	1:00	10:07	"	"

regular windows at the stations that most Russians use, and foreigners pay a higher price for train tickets than do Russians. Bring your passport, visa, or some other form of ID when you buy tickets so that the clerks can copy your name onto your ticket. It is usually impossible to buy round-trip tickets, though in summer 1996 it was sometimes possible to get return tickets from St. Petersburg by coming at least five days in advance.

Train Ticket Exceptions
Another way to get Tallinn or St. Petersburg tickets: The Intourist windows 19 and 20 (daily approximately 6:00–24:00, on the second floor of Leningradskii Vokzal at Metro: Komsomolskaya/Комсомольская) sell tickets to Tallinn and St. Petersburg for trains leaving *the same day or the next day only*. In 1996, their prices were slightly higher than at the Central Railway Agency. Go in the main hall of the station, then up the stairs in the far right corner of the hall, through the door on your right, and then to the left.

Same-day or next-day tickets to Helsinki: These are available *only* at windows 35 and 36 in a small special office on the first floor of Leningradskii Vokzal, on the left as you walk into the station's main hall (daily 8:00–13:00, 14:00–18:30). It is cheaper and not much slower to take the train to Tallinn and then the boat to Helsinki. It's also slightly cheaper to go by train to St. Petersburg and then on to Helsinki. If you must take the train to Helsinki, it's more convenient to buy tickets in advance from one of the four Central Railway Agency offices.

By Air

Connections between the Airport and Downtown: A taxi to or from Moscow's Sheremetyevo-2 Airport will run you at least $25 and possibly $40. If you can carry your luggage, the alternative is a bus-metro combination which costs pennies. Bus #551, and a faster "Express" bus on the same route, runs between Sheremetyevo and Metro: Rechnoi Vokzal/Речной Вокзал, the northern terminus of the green Metro line. The Express bus fare is just under $1, and bus #551 just requires Moscow bus tickets. The bus stop at Sheremetyevo-2 is a short walk out from the terminal, near the parking lot, past the taxi-Mafia gauntlet. The trip to Rechnoi Vokzal can take up to 45 minutes, a half-hour if you catch the express. Allow at least another 45 minutes on the Metro. These buses also service the domestic Sheremetyevo-1 terminal on the other side of the runways; don't get off here.

For booking and reconfirmation: British Airways, Krasnopresnenskaya naberezhnaya 12, #1905, tel. 253-2492; Delta, Krasnopresnenskaya naberezhnaya 12 #1102a, tel. 258-2658 or 258-2659; Finnair, Kamergerskii pereulok 6, tel. 292-8788 or 292-3337; LOT, Korovii val 7, tel. 238-0003 or 238-0313; Lufthansa, Olymic Penta Hotel, Olympiiskii Prospekt 18/1, tel. 975-2501; Malev, Kamergerskii pereulok 6, tel. 292-0434 or 229-3515; SAS, Kuznetskii Most 3, tel. 925-4747.

ST. PETERSBURG

Once a swamp, then an imperial capital, and now a showpiece of vanished aristocratic opulence shot through with the grimy ruins of socialism, St. Petersburg is Russia's most accessible and most tourist-worthy city. Standing in Palace Square, you'll shiver and think, "The revolution started here." (You may also shiver and think, "I'm as far north as Alaska.") Palaces, gardens, statues, and arched bridges over graceful canals bring back the time of the czars. Two of the world's greatest art museums top it off. Amid such artistic and historical splendor, modern Russia and its problems seem terribly out of place, but here they are: streets of legless beggars, Mafia-controlled kiosks, wheezing buses, shabby bread stores, broken signs, exhaust-stained facades, pornography dealers, and ice-cream stands in see-your-breath weather.

Compared to Moscow, St. Petersburg is compact, walkable, friendly, manageable, and architecturally intact. Don't get overly uptight about timing your visit to the summer solstice for St. Petersburg's much-bandied "White Nights." You'll be able to enjoy bright evenings here all summer long. If you want the real midnight sun, go to Finland.

Save a sunny day just to walk. Keep your head up: ugly Soviet shops mar the first floor of many buildings, but the upper facades are sun-warmed and untouched by street grime. Make sure you get off Nevsky Prospekt to explore the back streets along the canals. Visit the Summer Gardens. Climb St. Isaac's Cathedral for the view. The next day, when the Baltic Sea brings clouds and drizzle, plunge into the Hermitage or the Russian Museum.

Planning Your Time

Day 1
10:00 After breakfast, take a leisurely walk along Nevsky
      Prospekt to acquaint yourself with the city.
11:00 Climb up St. Isaac's Cathedral.
11:30 Walk back to Sadko's for lunch.
13:30 The Russian Museum is just up the street.
18:30 Take a taxi to the Korean House for dinner.

Day 2
10:30 Tour the Hermitage.
13:30 Have lunch at the Count Suvorov restaurant or Carrol's.
15:00 Take the Metro to the Peter and Paul Fortress.
18:30 Come back to the center for dinner at Tandoor.

St. Petersburg

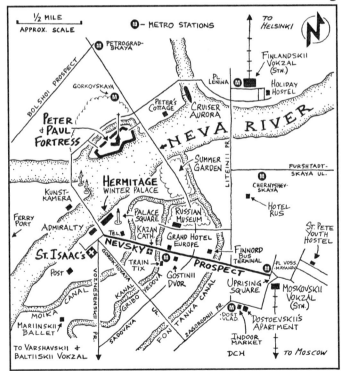

Day 3 (optional)
Spend more time in the Hermitage, visit the Piskaryovskoe
cemetery, or go to Petrodvorets for the day.

Orientation

Get to know Nevsky Prospekt (Невский Проспект), St.
Petersburg's main street. Almost everything you'll want to
see is either along Nevsky or between it and the river. A few
spots, like the Finland train station and the Peter and Paul
Fortress, are just across the river.

Nevsky starts at the slender-spired Admiralty, next to
the river and the Winter Palace. Running outward from the
city it crosses three canals: first the Moika (Мойка), then
Kanal Griboyedova (Канал Грибоедова), and finally the
Fontanka (Фонтанка). Tourist Nevsky ends a little farther
out at Ploshchad Vosstaniya (Uprising Square, Площадь
Восстания), home to a tall obelisk and the Moskovskii train
station.

Walking distances are manageable (from Ploshchad
Vosstaniya to the Admiralty takes only 30–45 minutes), and
St. Petersburg has enough natural landmarks that on a nice
summer day you can easily get around on foot without using
a map.

Tourist Information: Peter T.i.P.S., a private information office run by Westerners, is the closest thing to a tourist
information office that St. Pete has to offer (Monday–Friday
10:00–20:00, Saturday 12:00–18:00, Nevsky Prospekt 86,
located across from the Nevsky Palace Hotel, tel. 279-0037
or 275-0816, fax 275-0806, mailing address P.O. Box 109,
SF-53101 Lappeenranta, Finland). They give out tourist info
and book theater tickets, cruises, bus tours, homestays, and
hotel rooms. If you arrange accommodations in advance with
T.i.P.S., they will send you a visa support letter, and if you
want to visit Russian friends in St. Petersburg they will
arrange the visa for $55 which is much less bother than hav-
ing your friends work through OVIR.

English-language periodicals like *Pulse* and the *St. Petersburg Times*, which comes out on Tuesday and Friday, will
keep you up-to-date on events in the city.

American Embassy: Furshtadtskaya/Фурштадтская
ulitsa 15, Metro: Chernyshevskaya/Чернышевская, tel.
275-1701.

Bookstore: The **Mir** (Мир) international bookshop at Nevsky Prospekt 13, near Palace Square, has lots of new and used art books, English fiction (in the back room), and St. Petersburg maps at better prices than the outdoor stalls (Monday–Saturday 10:00–14:00 and 15:00–19:00).

Guides: Local guides are cheap, eager, and helpful. Try Alexandra Ivanova (who gives Hermitage tours, gets cheap tickets for concerts and ballets, and even takes people to the airport, $20/hr, tel. 232-6458 or 235-5062), and Alexy Alyoshetkin (who tailors sightseeing to your needs, tel. 543-8475).

Currency Exchange
5,000 rubles = about $1
It's available everywhere, though exchange offices are usually closed by 18:00 weekday evenings and all day on weekends. The American Express office is inside the Grand Hotel Europe (Monday–Friday 9:00–12:30 and 13:30–17:00, Saturday 9:00–13:00, Mikhailovskaya/Михайловская ulitsa 1, Metro: Nevsky Prospekt/Невский Проспект, tel. 329-6060). Their exchange desk is run by a Russian bank, not by Amex; at last report they took a 1 percent commission on traveler's checks. Emergency check cashing is available, but not cash advances.

Telephones and Mail
Brand-new, bright green card telephones have sprouted along the streets of St. Petersburg. Cards are available at shops and offices throughout the city—for example, at Peter T.i.P.S. The cheapest card costs about $6 for 100 units. For each minute, local calls cost 1 unit; to Moscow, 12 units; to the Baltics, 18; to Europe, 27; and to America, 63. The older public phones use the same tokens as the Metro.

You can also make long-distance calls at the central telephone office at Bolshaya Morskaya/Большая Морская ulitsa 5, between Palace Square and Nevsky Prospekt on the street with the big arches; look for the "PHONE" sign. For calls within the former Soviet Union, go to the right as you enter; a booth sells wide-grooved tokens for the intercity phones in the surrounding booths numbered 15–37 (open 24 hours daily). One 25-cent token buys 43 seconds to Moscow or 35 seconds to the Baltics. For international calls, go through the wooden gates on the left. Pick up a numbered token, go to the cabin with that number, make your call, and pay afterwards (open daily

St. Petersburg Metro

NOT TO SCALE

■ – TRANSFER STATIONS

ПЕТРОГРАДСКАЯ (PETROGRADSKAYA)

ГОРЬКОВСКАЯ (GORKOVSKAYA)

NEVA RIVER

ПЛ. ЛЕНИНА (PL. LENINA)

ПРИМОРСКАЯ (PRIMORSKAYA)

ГОСТИННЫЙ ДВОР (GOSTINY DVOR)

ЧЕРНЫШЕВСКАЯ (CHERNYSHEVSKAYA)

ВАСИЛЕОСТРОВСКАЯ (VASILEOST ROVSKAYA)

НЕВСКИЙ ПРОСПЕКТ (NEVSKY PROSPECT)

МАЯКОВСКАЯ (MAYAKOVSKAYA)

ПЛ. ВОССТАНИЯ (PL. VOSSTANIYA)

НОВОЧЕРКАССКАЯ (NOVOCHERKASSKAYA)

ДОСТОЕВСКАЯ (DOSTOEVSKAYA)

СЕННАЯ (SENNAYA)

САДОВАЯ (SADOVAYA)

ВЛАДИМИРСКАЯ (VLADIMIRSKAYA)

ПЛ. АЛЕКСАНДРА НЕВСКОГО (PL. ALEXANDRA NEVSUOGO)

ТЕХНОЛОГИЧЕСКИЙ ИНСТИТУТ (TECHNOLOGICHESKY INSTITUT)

ЛИГОВСКИЙ ПРОСПЕКТ (LIGOVSKY PROSPECT)

БАЛТИЙСКАЯ (BALTIISKAYA)

to МОСКОВСКАЯ (MOSKOVSKAYA) + AIRPORT BUSES

НАРВСКАЯ (NARVSKAYA)

— ESSENTIAL METRO WORDS —
- ENTRANCE – ВХОД
- EXIT (to CITY) – ВЫХОД (В ГОРОД)
- TRANSFER – ПЕРЕХОД
- WHERE IS... – ГДЕ...

8:00–23:00). Calls to America cost about $2.90/minute; to Europe, $1.30/minute. On most phones at this office you have to push the "Ответ" button when the other side answers.

The central post office is at Pochtamtskaya/Почтамтская ulitsa 9, under the arch a couple of blocks down from St. Isaac's Cathedral. Send international mail from window 25 (Monday–Saturday 9:00–19:30, Sunday 10:00–17:00).

Getting Around St. Petersburg

The Metro is not that helpful for getting around the center of the city, but essential for longer trips. It requires metal tokens which you can buy at station entrances for 20 cents and which also work in the pay phones. Trams and buses can be quite useful, but it takes some time to familiarize yourself with stops and routes. Buy yourself a street map. The Mir bookstore at Nevsky 13 has the best selection, but you can also try the Dom Knigi bookstore at Nevsky 28, or street stalls.

Taxis are a good option in St. Petersburg. You should pay the ruble equivalent of about $2 for an average trip within the center. Pay $1 if it's just a hop, skip, and a jump. Longer trips will run $3–$5. Some cabs are official and use the meter.

Unofficial cab drivers around major tourist sights may try to rip you off; refuse any driver who asks for payment in dollars.

Sights—St. Petersburg

▲▲▲**The Hermitage** (Эрмитаж)—The Hermitage's vast collection of European masters makes it one of the world's top art museums, ranking up there with the Louvre and the Prado. Some people come to Russia just to see this place. Others don't want to spend time on painters whose work can be admired more easily in New York, Paris, or Madrid. The first sort of person could spend days inside without exhausting the Hermitage's treasures; the second might want to bypass the place entirely in favor of the Russian Museum (see below) or no museums at all.

Here's a middle strategy. First, pick *one* artistic period that you really like, and head straight for that. Modern art is on the top floor, antiquities at ground level, and everything in between on the second floor.

Second, visit rooms 188–198 on the second floor, where the attraction is history, not art. Russian royalty once partied and feasted in these begilded, bedraped, and bejeweled chambers. In 1917, the Provisional Government met for the very last time in the green-pillared Malachite Hall (room 198), before being arrested in the adjacent dining room. The building faces Palace Square, where Bolshevik forces assembled before storming in.

The museum is in the czars' old Winter Palace, the green-and-white building between Palace Square and the river. The museum entrance is on the other, riverfront side of the building ($8, Tuesday–Saturday 10:30–18:00, Sunday 10:30–17:00, closed Monday, ticket windows close an hour before the museum, top floor closes 40 minutes early).

The number of people employed at the Hermitage is amazing—practically each one of the hundreds of rooms has an attendant.

▲▲**Russian Museum** (Русский Музей)—Here's a fascinating collection of prerevolutionary Russian art, particularly 18th- and 19th-century painting and portraiture. People who complain that the Hermitage is just more Monets and Rembrandts love the Russian Museum, since the artists are less well-known in the West. Much of the work reveals Russians exploring their own landscape: marshes, birch stands, muddy village streets, the conquest of Siberia, and firelit scenes in family huts. You'll see Repin's portrait of Tolstoy standing barefoot in the woods. You may enjoy Rerikh, an early 20th-century Russian artist who painted startling, imaginary, Himalayan landscapes in icy blue colors, or Vrubel's painting of *The Russian Hero*. Use either the main entrance, closer to the medieval art, or the side door along Kanal Griboyedova, closer to the early 20th-century paintings ($7, students $3.50, guided tours $20, free the first Wednesday of every month; Wednesday–Sunday 10:00–18:00, Monday 10:00–17:00, closed Tuesday; ticket window closes an hour before the museum; Inzhenernaya/ Инженерная ulitsa 4, a block off Nevsky behind the Grand Hotel Europe).

▲▲▲**Churches**—Russian Orthodox churches are reopening all over St. Petersburg and Moscow. When you see onion domes, walk in. Smaller churches are full of Russians morning, noon, and night, and will give you more of a feeling for Russian religion than will church-museums like St. Isaac's or the Kazan Cathedral. Plus, entrance is free, though you can leave a small donation towards renovation, or buy and light a candle. In St. Petersburg, there's a nice church at Vladimirskaya/ Владимирская metro, across from the indoor market, and another at the south end of Mokhovaya/Моховая ulitsa, by the first bridge across the Fontanka going north from Nevsky. For the best Orthodox service in St. Petersburg, take the Metro to ploshchad Aleksandra Nevskovo (Пл. Александра Невского) and attend the church in the *lavra* (seminary) across the street from the Metro exit, either on Sunday morning or for evening services daily at 18:00. It doesn't cost anything, unless you want to see Dostoevsky's grave in the cemetery across from the lavra (entrance $1).

▲▲**St. Isaac's Cathedral** (Исаакиевский Собор)—Head down Malaya Morskaya/Малая Морская ulitsa from Nevsky Prospekt. Your mission, should you decide to accept it, is to climb the colonnade stairway to the roof. The view is worth the climb and the money. Russians buy tickets at the booth outside the fence; foreigners have to go to the desk just inside the door. The inside of St. Isaac's is a museum, not a functioning church, and at $8 for the museum, $3 for the colonnade (students $4 and $1), I'd simply take a peek at the massive 19th-century interior while you buy your cheaper colonnade ticket. You can (and should) visit a real Russian house of worship for nothing (Thursday–Tuesday 11:00–18:00, last entry at 17:00, closed Wednesday).

▲**Kazan Cathedral** (Казанский Собор)—Reopened after years as a Museum of Atheism, this huge brown cathedral is on Nevsky at Kanal Griboyedova. It's not quite yet a functioning church either, but entrance is free (daily 9:00–20:00); one wing houses a museum of the history of religion ($3, students $1.50, Thursday–Tuesday 11:00–17:00, closed Wednesday).

▲▲**Nevsky Prospekt itself**—Nevsky's architectural highlights include the magnificent arch of the General Staff Building down Bolshaya Morskaya ulitsa, the Kazan Cathedral, and the views down the canals. You should also check out the sign at Nevsky 14, preserved from World War II, warning citizens that the north side of the street was more dangerous during shelling. The building with the distinctive tower at #28 is the city's main Dom Knigi (bookstore), formerly the Russian headquarters of the Singer sewing machine company.

▲**Peter and Paul Fortress** (Петропавловская Крепость)—Founded by Peter the Great in 1703 during the Great Northern War with Sweden, this fortress on an island in the Neva was the birthplace of the city of St. Petersburg. Its gold steeple catches the sunlight, and the blank walls face the Winter Palace across the river. You can wander through and climb the bastions for free. Your ticket lets you into the church (where Peter is buried), the jail (which housed numerous 19th-century revolutionaries including Lenin's older brother), and several museum-style exhibits. The main entrance is through the park from Metro: Gorkovskaya/Горьковская. Buy tickets inside the museum gift shop opposite the church, or from the "касса" to your right after you cross the bridge onto the island ($3, students half-price, Thursday–Monday 11:00–18:00, entry until 17:00, Tuesday 11:00–17:00, entry until 16:00; closed Wednesday and the last Tuesday of each month).

Moored in the river along Petrogradskaya nab. not far from the fortress is the Cruiser *Aurora* (Крейсер "Аврора"), which fired the shot that signaled the start of the Russian Revolution. Now a museum, it's worth visiting if you are a history buff or a Bolshevik, and with the Lenin Museum in Moscow closed, the *Aurora* now has one of Russia's best collections of Soviet kitsch (free, Tuesday–Thursday and Saturday–Sunday 10:30–16:00, closed Wednesday, no English descriptions).

Halfway between the Peter and Paul fortress and the

Nevsky Prospekt

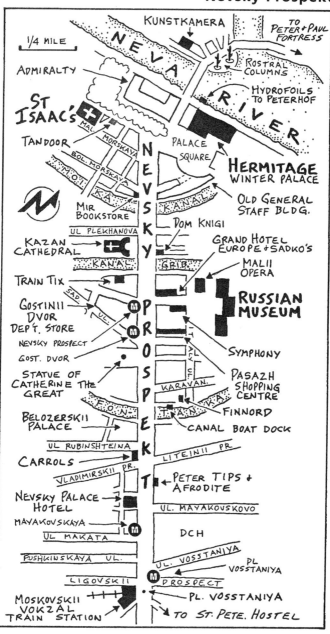

Aurora, at Petrovskaya nab. 6, is Peter the Great's log cabin, entombed in a small 19th-century brick house in a tiny park. Peter lived here briefly in 1703. The cabin may still be under renovation in 1997.

▲**Dostoevski Museum** (Музей Ф. М. Достоевского)—Although much of the furnishings are gone, you can get some feel for how the famous writer lived from visiting the six-room apartment where he wrote *The Brothers Karamazov*. Duck when you enter. Captions are in English. The *babushki* who run the place put a new half-cup of tea on Dostoevski's desk every morning ($2.50, students $1.25, Tuesday–Sunday 11:00–18:30, last entry 17:30, closed Monday and the last Wednesday of every month; Kuznechii/Кузнечый pereulok 5, a block from Metro: Dostoevskaya/Достоевская).

▲**Piskaryovskoe Memorial Cemetery** (Пискарёвское Мемориальное Кладбище)—This is a memorial to the hundreds of thousands who died in the city during the German siege of Leningrad in World War II. The cemetery, with its eternal flame, acres of mass grave bunkers (marked only with the year of death), moving statue of Mother Russia, and many pilgrims bringing flowers to remember lost loved ones, is an awe-inspiring experience even for an American tourist to whom the siege of Leningrad is just another page from the history books. To reach the cemetery, take the Metro north to Ploshchad Muzhestva (Площадь Мужества), exit, walk through the large brick apartment complex to the street, cross it to the eastbound bus stop, and take bus #123 to the sixth stop—you'll see the buildings on your left.

▲**Kunstkamera** (Кунсткамера)—This is officially known as the Peter the Great Museum of Anthropology and Ethnography. Truthfully, though, most people come only for the collection of hideously deformed preserved fetuses that Peter the Great bought from an Amsterdam doctor and had brought back to Russia. The rest is a vast, dusty, poorly-lit collection of Soviet-era dioramas and displays on world cultures. Check out the excellent American Indian section, the "Our Baltic Neighbors" display, or the selection of photographs of socialist Africa's public buildings. No English captions. ($2, Friday–Wednesday 11:00–18:00, entrance until 16:45, closed Thursday, Universitetskaya naberezhnaya 3, in the blue-and-white building across the big bridge from the Hermitage.)

▲▲Ballet, Opera, and Music—Keep an eye out for ballet and opera performances, advertised on posters all around town. The Marinskii (formerly Kirov) Ballet performs in Teatralnaya Ploshchad (Театральная Площадь), a little ways southwest of Nevsky—you may need to take a taxi. More convenient is the Malii Opera (Театр оперы и балета), which also has ballet, at ploshchad Isskustv/Исскуств 1, by the Russian Museum. The symphony is on Mikhailovskaya/Михайловская ulitsa across the street from the Grand Hotel Europe; the box office is next door. The theaters in St. Petersburg have cleaned up their act and scalpers have become extinct. Just go to the box office for tickets (usually open daily 11:00–19:00; closed for a lunch break at 14:00 or 15:00). The most popular ballets sell out a few days in advance, but for others there are seats left the day of the performance. At the Malii, foreigners pay about $25 for the nicest seats, less than $5 in the upper balconies. Symphony tickets are always cheaper. If you don't want to brave the box office, your hostel or hotel may be able to help you with tickets.

▲Boat trips—From June into September, trips on the St. Petersburg canals leave every half-hour from a dock on the Fontanka at Nevsky Prospekt (about $8).

▲▲Peterhof (Петергоф)—If you have time for a day trip, go to Peter the Great's lavish palace at Peterhof, also known as Petrodvorets (Петродворец), along the Gulf of Finland west of the city. This is Russia's Versailles and the target of many tour groups and travel poster photographers. Promenade along the grand canal, which runs through landscaped grounds from the boat dock up to the terraced fountains in front of the palace. There are ice cream stands aplenty and a nice indoor café with coffee and pastries. You can visit the museum inside the palace for $3, but it's more fun to stay outdoors. Children love to run past the so-called trick fountains—sometimes they splash you, sometimes they don't. In summer, "Meteor" hydrofoils leave for Peterhof every half-hour during the daytime from a dock across from the Hermitage entrance (30–40 min. trip, $8 each way, plus $6 entry to the palace grounds). In winter, you have to take a suburban train and then switch to a bus—ask for details (Tuesday–Sunday 11:00–8:00, closed Monday and last Tuesday of month).

Sleeping in St. Petersburg

(If calling from the U.S., dial 011-7-812, then the local number; for more phone info, see the Appendix: Direct Dialing Within the Baltics & Russia.)

Hostels

St. Petersburg International Hostel is a normal hostel like those in Western Europe, with friendly English-speaking staff, 60 beds in clean three- to five-bed rooms with clean showers, hot water year-round, a members' kitchen, a small shop, a cybercafé for Internet addicts, and Western movies every night. Seventeen dollars a night (hostel members $15) includes a continental breakfast (credit cards accepted). They're busy in summer, so reserve ahead by phone (tel. 329-8018, fax 329-8019, E-mail ryh@ryh.spb.su) or through the hostel's American office, listed below.

At 3rd Sovetskaya/3я Советская ulitsa 28, the hostel is about a ten-minute walk from Nevsky Prospekt, Ploshchad Vosstaniya, the Moskovskii Vokzal (train station), and the associated Metro stations. Coming out the front door of the train station, walk right, heading into the major street with overhead trolley wires. Take your first left off this street onto Suvorovskii/Суворовский prospekt. Walk 2 blocks (past the blue signs of the Philips housewares store) and then turn right onto 3rd Sovetskaya ulitsa. The hostel is the remodeled cream-and-magenta building half a block down on your left.

Downstairs you'll see Sindbad Travel, a fully accredited budget and student travel agency like STA and Council Travel in the U.S. Run by the hostel, Sindbad sells train and air tickets at fair prices (Monday–Friday 9:00–17:00, tel. 327-8384, fax 329-8019, E-mail sindbad@ryh.spb.su).

The best thing about the St. Petersburg International Hostel is its efficient system of visa support. If you're in the U.S.A. or Canada, the St. Petersburg Hostel office in Redondo Beach, California, will take your reservations and get your visa for you. Outside the U.S.A. or Canada, contact the hostel through its Internet site (http://www.spb.su/ryh/), through STA Travel, or through the Hostelling International booking network. Once you send all your details to the hostel (see below), they will send you a confirmation voucher and your visa support letter, which you can take or send to the nearest Russian consulate or embassy to get your visa. If you go through the California office, they'll get your visa for you too. You will usually receive visa support for ten days longer than you plan to stay in the hostel, which gives you the flexibility to stay longer without ridiculous extension hassles. The hostel can also provide one-year multiple-entry visas for $320.

The hostel will also take reservations for Holiday Hostel in St. Petersburg, the Travellers Guest House and Heritage Hostel in Moscow, and any future hostels that may open in Russia (there are plans for one in Irkutsk) and give visa support for your time there. In the summer they can get busy; if there's no room left they will confirm you for Holiday Hostel.

The hostel's mailing address is P.O. Box 8, SF-53501 Lappeenranta, Finland, but it's faster to contact them by fax, phone, or E-mail (see above). Their Worldwide Web address is http://www.spb.su/ryh/.

The hostel's handy American office is at 409 N. Pacific Coast Highway, Bldg. #106, Suite 390, Redondo Beach, CA 90277 (tel. 310/379-4316, fax 310/379-8420, E-mail 71573.2010@compuserve.com). Upon request, they will mail you a reservation form and information package. To get your Russian visa, they charge a $15 reservation fee, a $30 visa service fee, and as little as $40 for your visa (more if you need it quickly). You'll also pay $17 for each night you plan to stay at the hostel. You should plan to work at least four weeks in advance; faster processing is possible but more expensive.

If you are contacting the hostel directly by fax or E-mail, it will save time if your first communication includes your full legal name; citizenship; birthdate; passport number and expiration date; dates you plan to stay at the hostel; place, date, and means of entry into Russia; place, date, and means of exit from Russia; location of the Russian consulate where you plan to have your visa processed; Visa or MasterCard number; your name as it is written on the credit card; card expiration date; and signature. They need this information to make up your visa support letter and confirmation voucher. The hostel will charge you $52 ($25 for visa support, $10 fax fee, and $17 for your first night's stay at the hostel).

The hostel has a close relationship with Eurohostel in Helsinki—you can easily make reservations for the St. Pete's hostel when you're at the Helsinki hostel.

Holiday Hostel has more doubles and more congenial common space, and has a nicer view than the International

Hostel. On the other hand, the bathrooms are not as modern, the door is harder to find and get into, the hostel is not as tightly run, and it is beyond walking distance from Nevsky Prospekt (ulitsa Mikhailova/Михайлова 1, tel. 542 7364, fax 325-8559, E-mail postmaster@hostelling.spb.su). Holiday Hostel has about 100 beds in two- to six-bed rooms on several floors of a larger building, and charges $16–$19 per person per night, depending on the season. Breakfast is included and laundry service is available. Visa and MasterCard accepted.

The hostel is less than a five-minute walk from the Ploshchad Lenina (Площадь Ленина) Metro station at the Finlyandskii Vokzal (train station). Coming out the front door of the Metro station, walk straight down through the park to the river, then turn left 1 block to ulitsa Mikhailova; the hostel is in the building on the far left corner with the fourth-floor corner balcony. The hostel entrance is in the inside corner of the L-shaped building; go in through the archway off of ulitsa Mikhailova, look for the "YH" sign on the wall, and ring the bell—the hostel is on the third floor. (You can't get in yourself without punching in the code they'll give you.) We advise reserving at Holiday Hostel through the Russian Youth Hostels office in California, but Holiday Hostel can also provide independent visa support by fax; visit their Internet home page at http://www.spb.su/holiday/index.html.

Hotels

The St. Petersburg hotel scene is frustrating. The cheaper hotels—with doubles under $50—are usually too sleazy or too far from the Metro. Hotels with new furniture, appealing bathrooms, and a modern lobby start at $100 for a double, and even that often means a pompous Soviet-style reception desk, congealed breakfast, distant location, shady characters in the lobby, and $40,000 cars (without license plates) parked outside. What's more, these hotels generally aren't together enough to fax you an invitation letter to support your visa application. For enlightened service, propriety, and visa support in the center of the city, there are first-world fortresses such as the Nevsky Palace (tel. 311-6366), the Grand Hotel Europe (329-6000), and the Astoria (311-4206), but they cost upwards of $200 a night. Here are a few places worth recommending:

The cheapest of the high-price hotels (though its rooms are correspondingly small—it's a ship, after all) is the Swiss-run

Hotelship Peterhof, moored at naberezhnaya Makarova 24 (tel. 325-8888, fax 325-8889), where double rooms start at $190 (reserve at 415/398-7947 in the U.S.A.).

If you're booking a flight-plus-hotel package from Finnair or another tour operator, the **Hotel Deson-Ladoga** (Десон-Ладога) is a safe bet: the rooms are nice, the reception staff is young and speaks English, it's only a block from the Novocherkasskaya metro, and it's possible to get doubles for less than $100 through Peter T.i.P.S. or through a tour operator (prospekt Shaumyana/Шаумяна 26, tel. 528-5200, fax 528-5448).

If you're already in Russia, don't need visa support, and are just looking for a cheap, central, livable hotel with private facilities, try the **Hotel Rus** (Гостиница Русь), on a quiet street just blocks from Nevsky Prospekt (Artilleriiskaya/ Артиллерийская ulitsa 1, Metro: Chernyshevskaya/ Чернышевская, tel. 273-4683). Built for the 1980 Olympics, it's definitely one of the world's ugliest hotels, but the rooms are standard and the lobby is surprisingly welcoming. Doubles with bath run about $50; the bathrooms are typically Soviet, but OK.

Private Rooms

An organization which has been around for several years and which seems reliable is the **Host Family Association,** which sets up homestays with families in St. Petersburg for $50–$60/day per two persons, $100 with all meals. Contact them by E-mail at alexei@hofak.hop.stu.neva.ru, or use tel./fax 7/812/275-1992 in St. Petersburg. They meet you at the train or the airport and bring you to your hosts' apartment. Another homestay organization is the **Russia Experience** (USA contact: Petit Travel Consultants, tel. 800/683-7403, fax 508/792-0065).

White Nights (Belije Nochi) is a small company with offices in St. Louis and St. Petersburg which arranges homestays (about $25/night with breakfast) and hotels in St. Petersburg and Moscow with visa support (about $25/night with breakfast). They also specialize in kayak trips, trans-Siberian train tickets, and getting travelers way out in the Russian toolies. Contact their St. Louis office at tel./fax 314/991-5512, E-mail russiawnights@arcom.sbbsv, or on the web at http://www.concourse.net/bus/wnights/.

Eating in St. Petersburg

The listings below are your best bets for good food served honestly for $10–$15 a meal.

At **Koreiskii Domik** (Корейский Домик, i.e., Korean House), a full meal runs about $12 per person, including tea, rice, spicy pickled vegetables, and an entreé like *chapche* (noodles with vegetables and meat), *lapsha* (noodles and meat in broth), or *pulgogi* (spicy Korean-style meat cooked on a burner on your table). Quick service, English menu. And we've had their filtered water and never gotten sick. In summer especially, try to reserve at tel. 259-9333 (daily 13:00–22:00). It's at Izmailovskii/Измайловский prospekt 2, at the intersection with the Fontanka canal and near the blue-domed church; the entrance is on Izmailovskii. It's easiest to taxi there along the Fontanka, but you can get there by foot in 15–20 minutes from Metro: Tekhnologicheskii Institut/Технологический Институт: walk west on 1я Красноармейская to Izmailovskii, then take a right to the canal.

Sadko's, the cheapest of the three restaurants in the Grand Hotel Europe, is St. Petersburg's yuppie American hangout. Inside it feels like Manhattan. The menu is chalked on blackboards, and parts of it vary daily. Main dishes cost about $10–$15; desserts (they have great cakes) go for $4–$6. Beverages are expensive (Cokes, $3). Visa, MasterCard, and Amex accepted. No non-smoking section. Live music every evening after about 9:00 or 10:00. Ask a lady at the bar what her name is, and she'll answer "$200." (Daily 12:00–01:00, last orders at 00:30; at the corner of Nevsky Prospekt and ulitsa Mikhailovskaya/Михайловская, almost across the street from Gostinii Dvor, tel. 329-6000 for reservations.)

Restaurant Tandoor serves normal Indian food near St. Isaac's Cathedral for about $15 per person. Service could be faster and portions larger, but for St. Petersburg it's not bad, and the staff speaks English and accepts credit cards (Voznesenskii/Вознесенский prospekt 2, at the corner of Admiralteiskii prospekt, tel. 312-3886, daily 12:00–23:00).

Carrol's (Кэрролс), Nevsky 45 at the corner of ulitsa Rubinshteina, serves the best fast food in the center—a burger, fries, and Coke for about $4. Another branch is at ulitsa Vosstaniya 3, near the Moscow Station (daily 9:00–23:00).

Count Suvorov (Графъ Суворовъ) is a not-bad place to get real Russian food for lunch in between a day's sightseeing.

For about $12 you can get, for example, borscht, chicken Kiev, and your choice of "garnishes" (potato, cauliflower, or French fries) beautifully presented on big plates in this small, modern restaurant near the south end of the Gostinii Dvor department store (ulitsa Lomonosova/Ломоносова 6, daily 12:00–24:00, tel. 315-4328).

Kavkaz (Кавказ) is a good Georgian restaurant which you should try if you won't make it to Moscow (see our Georgian food ordering guide in the Moscow section). A meal in the restaurant section will run you $15–$20. There's also a café section (right on the corner of the street) with the same food for much lower prices (e.g., *khachapuri* costs less than a dollar for a quarter-pie). Avoid the "Georgian national soup" (*khashi*). Take the metro to Novocherkasskaya/Новочеркасская, then walk downhill towards the river and the bridge 1 block; it's on the far right corner (ulitsa Stakhanovtsev/Стахановцев 5, tel. 221-4309, restaurant open daily 12:00–23:00, café open Monday–Saturday 9:00–21:00, Sunday 10:00–19:00).

In summer the Afrodite restaurant at Nevsky 86 runs a **beer garden** in its courtyard (go through the archway; daily 12:00–01:00).

La Cucuracha is a Mexican restaurant staffed by Cubans with $6 enchiladas (naberezhnaya Reki Fontanki 39, a block and a half south of Nevsky along the inner side of the Fontanka, open Sunday–Thursday 12:00–01:00, Friday–Saturday 12:00–05:00, tel. 110-4006).

The St. Petersburg **bar scene** centers around Galernaya/Галерная ulitsa, near St. Isaac's. Two popular places are **Senat**, at Galernaya 1, and **Tribunal**, at Senatskaya ploshchad 1.

Picnics

Farmer's market: A trip here will show you the true scope of Russia's agricultural richness (and fill your picnic basket). St. Petersburg's best and most central farmer's market is at Kuznechii/Кузнечый pereulok, right across the street from the Dostoevski museum (look for the big Рынок sign; Metro: Vladimirskaya/Владимирская). Any Russian farmer's market is worth a visit even if you're not shopping. First you'll pass babushki selling plastic bags, then Georgians shouting *"Molodoi chelovyek!"* (young man) and *"Devushka!"* (young lady) as they try to entice you towards their piles of oranges,

tomatoes, cucumbers, and pears. In the honey (Мёд) section,
a chorus line of white-aproned babushki stands ready to let
you dip and test each kind. Check out the barrels of sauerkraut and trays of pickled garlic and cabbage. In the herbs
section, you can sniff massive bunches of fresh coriander
(кинза) and wade through a lifetime of horseradish (хрен);
nearby, look for a Central Asian spice trader with wares of
every color laid out in little bags. (Monday–Saturday
8:00–19:00, Sunday 8:00–16:00, closed one Monday a month
for cleaning.)

Grocery stores: There are now small markets in every
neighborhood where you can pick up bread, fruit, bottled
water, Finnish or Estonian milk, cheese, and yogurt, and other
necessities. If you need to do a major shopping, the Finnish
chain **Stockmann** has a store at Finlyandskii/Финляндский
prospekt 1 (daily 10:00–21:00), across the street from the
round building of the Hotel St. Petersburg and across the
Sampsonievskii Most (bridge) from the Cruiser *Aurora*. This is
about three stops on tram #6 from either Metro:
Gorkovskaya/Горьковская or Ploshchad Lenina/Площадь
Ленина, or you can walk.

Transportation Connections—St. Petersburg

By Train
Stations: Trains to Moscow leave from the Moskovskii Vokzal
(Московский Вокзал, Moscow Station, Metro: Ploshchad
Vosstaniya/Площадь восстания).

Trains to the Baltics leave from the Varshavskii Vokzal
(Варшавский Вокзал, Warsaw Station). Metro:
Baltiiskaya/Балтийская brings you to the nearby (and confus-
ingly named) Baltiiskii Vokzal; from the Metro exit, walk to
the main street, turn right, and walk 1 long block to the Varshavskii Vokzal.

Trains to Helsinki leave from Finlyandskii Vokzal
(Финляндский Вокзал, Finland Station, Metro: Ploshchad
Lenina/Площадь Ленина).

Buying Tickets: Tickets for all trains are available without too much hassle at the Central Railway Booking Office
(Monday–Saturday 8:00–20:00, Sunday 8:00–16:00, Kanal Gri-
boyedova/Канал Грибоедова 24). This is across the canal from
the Kazan Cathedral and just a few doors from Nevsky

Trains Departing St. Petersburg

#	To	Departs	Arrives	2nd Class	1st Class
37	Riga (Рига)	21:40	8:00	$37	$68
649	Tallinn (Таллинн)	22:57	8:04	$21	$36
191	Vilnius (Вильнюс)	23:27	12:26	$33	$60
33*	Helsinki (хельсинки)	8:10	14:03	$51	$90
35**	"	16:00	21:34	$51	$82
23	Moscow (Москва)	13:05	21:55	$32	$57
159	"	15:58	21:43	$41	$67
19	"	21:55	6:00	$32	$57
27	"	22:30	6:45	$32	$57
9	"	22:45	7:10	$41	$67
25	"	23:10	7:15	$32	$57
5	"	23:33	7:45	$32	$57
1	"	23:55	8:25	$41	$67
3	"	23:59	8:30	$32	$57
11	"	0:05	9:13	$32	$57
13	"	0:35	10:03	$32	$57

* Russian-run *Repin*
** Finnish-run *Sibelius*

Prospekt. Look for the steam engine sign above the building. Metro: Nevsky Prospekt/Невский Проспект.

Only Russian citizens are officially allowed to buy tickets from the windows in the main ground-floor hall. Foreigners should go to the right, through the door, and up the stairs next to the women's bathroom to the second floor, following the signs saying кассы международного сообщения. Most clerks do not speak English. They need to write your last name on the ticket in Cyrillic, and the easiest way to help them do this is to bring your passport and visa, but if you can't do that, any other ID (such as an American driver's license) is usually OK. Windows 100-104 sell advance and same-day tickets to foreigners for destinations within the former Soviet Union, including the Baltic states. Round-trip tickets (e.g., to Moscow) are difficult or impossible to get. Students at Russian universities can visit windows 101 and 102 for lower rates. Window 94 sells tickets to Finland. If you have questions, window 90 is for information (75 cents per visit). To get your money back on tickets you don't want, visit window 91. (These window numbers could change.)

If you don't want to brave the central booking office, Sindbad Travel at the St. Petersburg International Hostel can get tickets for you at a slight markup (see under Hostels, above).

St. Petersburg to Helsinki: The Finnish-run Sibelius afternoon train is far more convenient than the Russian Repin. It's sleek, blue, and comfortable, and you can just hop on board and pay the conductor with a credit card, or in dollars or Finnish marks (although it's preferable, and slightly cheaper, to come a little early and buy a ticket at window 10 in the station). Since the Sibelius arrives in Helsinki in the evening, you should try to set up a place to stay by phone while in St. Petersburg.

The Russian-run Repin is not as nice as the Sibelius, though the price is the same. Since it leaves before the ticket windows open in the morning and since you can't pay on board, you have to buy your ticket the day before or earlier.

You can buy tickets for both trains from special windows at Finlyandskii Station itself, either in advance or on the day of departure. Walk two car-lengths up platform 1 and go in the door marked "Train tickets Express-2" in English. Window 9 sells tickets for the Russian train; window 10 sells tickets for the Finnish train (both windows open Monday–Saturday 8:00–12:00 and 13:00–19:00, Sunday 8:00–12:00 and 13:00–16:00). As tickets on these trains almost never sell out, it's enough to come the day of departure (for the Finnish train) or the day before (for the Russian train). If you prefer, you can also get tickets for these trains at the Central Railway Booking Office, window 94 (though not on the day of departure).

St. Petersburg to Poland: There are daily direct trains from St. Petersburg to Warsaw and Berlin, but since these transit Latvia, Lithuania, and then Belarus, they are one long nightmare of customs and immigration checks, plus you may need various transit visas. Get to Poland instead from Moscow or the Baltics.

By Bus

St. Petersburg to Helsinki: The St. Petersburg Express Bus leaves St. Petersburg at 8:45 and arrives in Helsinki at 15:45. Pick-ups in St. Petersburg are at 8:00 at the Hotel Pulkovskaya (near Metro: Moskovskaya/Московская), and 8:25 at Hotel Astoria (across from St. Isaac's), and 8:45 at Grand Hotel Europe. Make reservations at the Sovauto desk in the lobby of the Pulkovskaya (tel. 264-5125), or just show up. The bus continues from Helsinki to Turku port, meeting the Turku-Stockholm overnight ferries. Tickets to Helsinki cost $51, students 10 percent off.

The Pietarin Linja bus leaves St. Petersburg at 12:00 and arrives in Helsinki at 19:35 (no advance booking office, just buy tickets from the driver). The bus departs daily from Hotel Moskva (Metro: pl. Aleksandra Nevskovo) at 12:00 and from the Hotel Astoria at 12:30. Tickets $46, students 10 percent off.

The Finnord bus leaves St. Petersburg at 15:30 and arrives in Helsinki at 22:15. It departs from the handy English-speaking office and waiting room at ulitsa Italyanskaya/Итальянская 37 (a half-block in from the Fontanka canal and a block from Nevsky Prospekt, Metro: Gostinii Dvor/Гостиныи Двор, tel. 314-8951, fax 314-7058 for reservations). Tickets $49, students 30 percent off.

St. Petersburg to Tallinn: Buses leave daily at 7:00 and 17:00 (arriving in Tallinn at 13:20 and 23:20) from platform 5 at Bus Station #2 (naberezhnaya Obvodnovo Kanala/Обводного Канала 36). Exit Metro: Ligovskii Prospekt/Лиговский Проспект, then go one tram stop south (just across the canal), and a block-and-a-half east along the canal. Or take a cab. Buy tickets inside the station for $11.

By Air

Connections between the Airport and Downtown: St. Petersburg's Pulkovo airport has two terminals. Pulkovo-I handles domestic flights and Pulkovo-II handles international flights. To reach either from downtown St. Petersburg, first take the Metro to the Moskovskaya/Московская station, take the exit on the outbound end of the station, and go all the way through the underground tunnel. This will bring you out next to the stops for bus #13 (which goes to Pulkovo-II) and bus #39 (which goes to Pulkovo-I). At peak times bus #13 runs every 20 minutes. Since Pulkovo-II is not the end of bus #13's route, there are both inbound and outbound bus stops at the airport (marked by yellow signs). If you've just landed and need to take the bus into town, stand at the inbound stop (near the arrivals hall).

For booking and reconfirmation: You can visit major airlines' downtown offices such as British Airways, Nevsky Prospekt 57, tel. 325-6222; Delta, Bolshaya Morskaya ulitsa 36, tel. 311-5820; Finnair, Malaya Morskaya ulitsa 19, tel. 315-9736; LOT, Karavannaya ulitsa 1, tel. 273-5721; Malev, Voznesenskii pr. 7, tel. 315-5455; Swissair and Austrian Air, Nevsky Prospekt 57, tel. 314-5086; SAS, Nevsky Prospekt 57, tel. 311-6112.

THE
BALTICS

TALLINN, ESTONIA

Tallinn is the flagship of Baltic reform. During the Soviet era, Tallinners spent their evenings watching Finnish television beamed across the gulf from Helsinki. When independence came, they knew exactly what a Western economy should look like. Since 1991 they've been putting one together as fast as possible. If only everyone in the ex-Soviet Union could learn from the Estonians.

Walk into any grocery store and you'll begin to understand. Tallinn has embraced the idea of the supermarket, where you pick food off the shelves yourself instead of asking clerks behind a counter to do it. The healthiest sign is that stores carry a sensible mix of imported and domestic goods, just like any other store in Europe. Estonian design has recovered from Sovietism: colorful, simple, Scandinavian layout is showing up in airline ads and yogurt packaging. And Estonia's competitive trade policy is producing competitive goods: while Russian exports to Estonia have sunk, in St. Petersburg you can now pick up Estonian orange juice, cucumbers, and frozen fish. This little country is succeeding.

Why the economic precociousness? One main reason is that Estonians consider their country a Nordic nation of solid, hardworking Protestant folk like those who made Scandinavia a showcase of order, propriety, and comfort. They're quick to point out that Finland and Estonia both gained independence from Russia after World War I, that as late as 1938, Estonia's living standard was equal to Finland's, and that Estonians would have kept pace had it not been for a couple hundred Russian tanks.

Of course, well-stocked grocery stores look perfectly normal if you come to Tallinn on the boat from Helsinki. This is why I suggest that you arrive in Tallinn from Russia or one of the other Baltic capitals. You'll feel like you're back in the West already. Coming from Helsinki, Tallinn looks run-down. Remember that it gets worse, and enjoy Tallinn while you can.

Planning Your Time
Tallinn deserves more time than Riga or Vilnius. But it's fairly small and its sights are modest. On a first trip, two days are plenty.

Day 1
11:00 Wander through the Old Town, looking out for concert posters on your way up to Toompea, Tallinn's fortified hill.
12:30 Leisurely lunch at Toomkooli.
14:00 Go down to Kiek in de Kök and see the photography exhibitions.
15:00 Explore the small galleries and shops in the Old Town. Stop in any café when you want a rest.
19:00 Concerts usually take place at this time. Come a little early for tickets.
20:30 Dinner at Eesli Tall.
22:00 Retire to Hell Hunt or the Eesli Tall cellar bar.

Day 2
10:00 Check out the Holy Ghost Church and perhaps the Tallinn Town Museum or the Estonian History Museum.
12:00 Assemble picnic fixings at the Kaubahall supermarket. Take the tram out to Kadriorg.
13:30 Picnic and walk through the Kadriorg park and palace grounds.
18:00 Return to the Old Town for dinner at Vanaema Juures (make reservations ahead of time).
20:00 Plenty of time for mulled wine at the Virgin Tower.

Orientation
Tallinn owes its existence to Toompea, the precipitous hill on which the city's Upper Town stands. Fortified by the Danes after they captured Tallinn in 1219, Toompea turned into

Tallinn Old Town

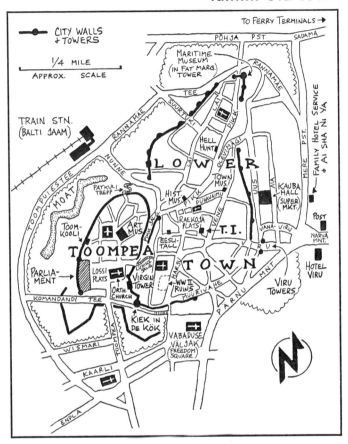

Tallinn's aristocratic neighborhood during the later Middle Ages—Toompea Castle still houses the Estonian government. Merchants and artisans, meanwhile, built the other half of old Tallinn, the Lower Town, beneath Toompea. Two steep, narrow streets—the "Long Leg" (Pikk jalg) and the "Short Leg" (Lühike jalg)—connect the two towns. Tallinn's intact city wall counts 29 watchtowers, each topped by a pointy red roof. Nineteenth- and early 20th-century architects circled the Old Town, putting up broad streets of public buildings, low Scandinavian-style apartment buildings, and single-family wooden houses. Soviet planners then ringed this with endless stands of crumbling concrete high-rises where many of Tallinn's Russian immigrants settled. The Town Hall Square (Raekoja plats), in the center of the Lower Town, is an important reference point.

Tourist Information: Tallinn's excellent, English-speaking tourist office has maps, concert listings, booklets, phrase books, postcards, and free brochures (Monday–Friday 9:00–19:00, Saturday–Sunday 10:00–17:00; closing an hour early off-season; on the main square, Raekoja plats 18, tel. 631-3940, fax 631-3941).

American Embassy: Kentmanni 20, third floor, tel. 631-2021.

Bookstore: Homeros carries books exclusively in foreign languages including English. It doesn't have a very big selection, but it's worth visiting (Monday–Friday 10:00–19:00, Saturday–Sunday 11:00–17:00; Vene 20).

Laundry: Seebimull Pesumaja, a self-service and drop-off laundromat, is at Liivalaia 7 (1 block east of Pärnu maan-tee at the intersection with Suda, tel. 2/682-010).

Currency Exchange

12 Estonian kroons (kr) = about $1, 1 kroon = 100 senti

There are booths everywhere. Banks have the best rates—look for a 1–1.5 percent spread between buying and selling prices. A 1 percent commission on traveler's checks is standard. A lot of change points, like those in major hotels, have very poor rates, so shop around. The American Express representative is at Suur-Karja 15 in the Old Town (Monday–Friday 9:00–18:00, Saturday 10:00–17:00).

Telephones and Mail

Both services are in the fortress-like building across Narva maantee from the Hotel Viru. Send letters from the second-floor post office (Monday–Friday 8:00–20:00, Saturday 9:00–17:00). For long-distance calls, the office on the lower floor of the post office building is open daily from 7:00–22:00. The best way to call is with phone cards (in 30kr, 50kr, and 100kr sizes) sold in the tele-phone office and around town. These work in Estonia's new card phones. Calls to Helsinki, Riga, and Vilnius cost 5kr per minute; to Russia and Sweden, 7.5kr; to America, 20kr. Tallinn's old pay phones (local calls only) take a 20-senti coin; local calls from a card-operated phone cost 23 senti.

Tallinn has two types of telephone numbers. The seven-digit ones have no area code and always begin with 6, like this: 632-3232. The six-digit numbers have an area code (2) which we always list before the number, like this: 2/454-454. Calling within the city, you dial all seven digits of the numbers that begin with 6, but only the last six digits of the numbers that begin with 2. Making a long-distance or international call to Tallinn, always dial the full seven numbers, including the 2 before six-digit numbers.

Getting Around Tallinn

Unless you're sleeping far from the center, you should be able to do most of your sightseeing on foot. Tallinn's trams are very simple and convenient. Check the map for route and stop locations. All trams meet in the center, by the Hotel Viru. They run until about midnight. One of the easiest ways to get around Tallinn is to spend $5 on a ten-day card (*10-päeva-kaart*) which gives you unlimited rides on public transport in Tallinn. Cards and tickets are sold at the kiosks by tram stops that say *sõiduta-longid* in the window. You can also get single tickets for 4kr from the booths or on board. Some buses are run by a private company called MRP (they have a three-triangle logo); these cost 5kr per ride and passes are not valid.

Taxis are cheap and handy in Tallinn. Always make sure to take an official taxi. The largest, cheapest, and most reliable taxi company is Tulika Takso; the best way to summon them is to call 639-5959.

Sights—Tallinn

Tallinn has no incredible sights which demand to be seen. Rather, it steadily delivers small and pleasing towers, museums, ramparts, facades, churches, and shops. Wander through the Old Town, have a Saku in the square, duck down every street and into every shop that looks interesting, and peer up at the Hanseatic facades and medieval towers.

▲▲▲**Toompea**—This is the fortified hill where Tallinn was founded in the 13th century and the Upper Town was built. Walk up Nunne tänav, the street that leads from the train station to the Old Town, then cut off to the right and climb up the stairs. The ramparts at the top reward you with a perfect photo opportunity of the Lower Town's red roofs and steeples. Wandering will bring you to the **Dome Church** (Toomkirik)

Tallinn

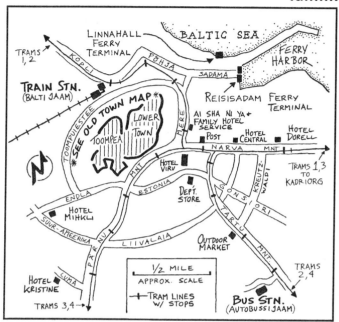

and eventually out to the square by the colorful **Russian Orthodox Church**, a plump, out-of-place, onion-domed edifice planted here after the Russian takeover of Tallinn in 1710. The interior is worth a peek.

Downhill from the church you'll see two towers. The square **Virgin Tower** (Neitsitorn) houses a café; the round one is **Kiek in de Kök** ("Peek in the Kitchen"), so named because one could supposedly spy on the Lower Town's residents from its heights. The top floor and the bottom two floors now house changing exhibits of the latest in Estonian photography, while in the middle you can see medieval cannons and charts left over from the Livonian wars (7kr, Tuesday–Friday 10:30–17:30, Saturday–Sunday 11:00–16:30). If you head back down to the Lower Town from here you'll pass by **St. Nicholas' Church** (Niguliste Kirik) and the World War II ruins behind it, left untouched as a memorial.

▲**Walking Tour**—You can hire a private walking tour of the Old Town. Just drop by the tourist office or the CDS office next door.

▲▲**Holy Ghost Church** (Pühavaimu Kirik)—This quintessentially northern 14th-century church has a fantastic old outdoor clock. Inside, hunched, whitewashed walls contrast with the faded medieval artwork on aged pews and galleries. Watch for periodic organ concerts (at Pühavaimu tänav and Pikk tänav across from the Maiasmokk café).

▲**Estonian History Museum** (Eesti Ajaloomuuseum)—Quite varied exhibits, so you may be able to find something to hold your interest among archaeology, military history, a roomful of domestic displays, and more. Look for the English captions on the sides of the glass cases. The building is Tallinn's 15th-century Great Guildhall (5kr, Thursday–Tuesday 11:00–18:00, closed Wednesday, Pikk 17, across from the Holy Ghost Church).

▲**Estonian Maritime Museum** (Eesti Meremuuseum)—Housed in the Paks Margareta ("Fat Margaret") tower, the museum itself is less interesting than the view of Tallinn's port if you go out the wooden door on the top floor and up to the tower roof. It's scary to think that anyone might have ever used the suit of copper diving armor, built by a Tallinner in the 1920s, that stands in a corner of the bottom floor (6kr, students 2kr, Wednesday–Sunday 10:00–18:00, closed Monday and Tuesday, Pikk 70).

▲**Estonian Art Museum** (Eesti Kunstimuuseum)—Shouldn't be your first stop in town, but if you're interested in late 19th- and early 20th-century art, go check out what the Estonians were doing. There's also a small case of avantgarde bookprinting from the 1920s (7 kr, Wednesday–Monday 11:00–17:30, closed Tuesday, Kiriku plats 1, on Toompca).

▲**Tallinn Town Museum** (Tallinna Linnamuuseum)—Features Tallinn history from 1700 to 1918, with the upstairs exhibit on Tallinn from 1900 to 1917 the best part. The mixture of Russian, German, and Estonian reminds us that the ethnic situation here was once even more complicated than it now is (5kr, students 2.50kr, Wednesday–Friday 10:30–17:30, Saturday–Sunday 10:30–16:30, closed Monday, Vene 17 at the corner of Pühavaimu).

▲▲**Kadriorg**—This seaside park and summer residence was built by Peter the Great for Catherine after Russia took over Tallinn in 1710. The mansion is now the home of the president of Estonia. The park, which runs down to the sea to the north, is the perfect spot for your picnic. Trams #1 and #3 go east from the center of town to Kadriorg at the end of the line. It's an easy 15-minute ride out and back.

▲▲▲**Estonian Music**—Tallinn has one of the densest per-capita schedules of Baroque, Renaissance, and choral music performances in Northern Europe. Estonian choral music got its first push from the long German Lutheran presence in Tallinn, and then became intimately bound up with the struggle for independence after the first Estonian Song Festival in 1869 (which is still held every five years). Even outside of festival times, it's a rare week in which there aren't a few performances in Tallinn's churches and concert halls, advertised on posters around town ("Hortus Musicus" is the name of Estonia's best-known Renaissance music performance group). In most cases tickets are available either at the door or in advance from the Eesti Kontsert ticket office inside the big theater (Monday–Saturday 13:00–19:00) at Estonia puiestee 4 across the park from the Hotel Viru. Estonian groups have put out a lot of good CDs, and the place to look for them is the record shop at Kuninga 4, around the corner from Raekoja plats (Monday–Friday 9:00–19:00, Saturday 9:00–17:00). Estonia's three best modern choral composers and arrangers are Arvo Pärt, Veljo Tormis, and Erkki-Sven Tüür.

▲▲**Artwork, handicrafts, and shopping**—With so many Scandinavian tourists coming to Tallinn now the Old Town is full of trinkets. For sweaters and woolens, try the **Gallerii Kaks** on the second floor of Lühike jalg 2 (daily 11:00–19:00). **Diele Gallerii** sells the best postcards in town, displays some drawings by the postmodern Estonian graphic artist Eduard Wiiralt (died 1953), and has some nice art for sale (at Vanaturu kael 3 just below Raekoja plats). Also check out the **Kinaver** ceramics store on Toompea at Pikk jalg 9, next to what must be the cleanest public bathrooms in the ex-Soviet Union. The **Tallinn Department Store** (Tallinna Kaubamaja) is behind the Hotel Viru (Monday–Saturday 9:00–20:00, Sunday 10:00–18:00) and the new Stockmann department store is a little farther away, on Liivalaia.

Sleeping in Tallinn

(12kr = about $1)

If you're calling from the U.S., dial 011-372, then the local number; for more phone info, see the Appendix: Direct Dialing Within the Baltics & Russia.

Respectable Hotels

Hotell Mihkli delivers actual respectability at the best rates in town. This means newish furniture, functioning bathrooms, locked parking, a TV, phone, and nice writing desk in every room, and a welcoming reception desk. Singles with breakfast and sauna included cost 480kr and doubles are 720kr. It's past the National Library a little outside the center, but not too far to walk. You can also take trolleybuses #2, #3, or #6; the hotel is by the "Koidu" stop (Endla 23, tel. 2/453-704, fax 2/451-767).

Hotell Central is a little more expensive, but the location lives up to the name and the rooms are very new. Singles are 800kr, doubles are 990kr, and breakfast is included (Narva maantee 7, tel. 633-9800, fax 633-9900).

Hotel Nepi is a small, friendly, family-run hotel a short bus ride from the center where singles with bath cost 400kr, doubles 550kr, and breakfast 50kr. It's about a 25kr taxi ride from the ferry port (at Nepi 10, tel. 655-1665, fax 655-1664).

Hotell Kristiine just makes it into the "respectable" category. This is the cheapest hotel in town where you can have a private bathroom. The rooms are standard-issue Soviet style on several floors of a taller building, well-kept but with older furniture, TVs, and telephones. Each room has a small, spartan private bathroom. The reception is well-organized and speaks English. Singles with bath and breakfast cost 260kr, doubles are 420kr, triples 540kr. Take tram #3 or #4 to the "Vineeri" stop at the corner of Pärnu maantee and Luha tänav; the hotel is about 3 blocks down Luha at #16 (tel. 2/682-000, fax 2/682-030).

Cheaper Hotels and Hostels

Hotell Dorell is a good choice for students: double rooms with clean shared bathrooms cost 300kr (breakfast not included). Not much English is spoken. Call ahead, because it's small. Take tram line #1 or #3 to the "Kreutzwaldi" stop, just east of the city center along Narva maantee. When you get off the tram, go through the archway at Narva maantee 23 and you'll see the hotel sign to your left (Karu 39, tel. 626-1200, fax 2/423-387).

The Barn (Hotell Küün), centrally located one block off the town square, is Tallinn's youth hostel. Everyone speaks English. There's space for 36 people in several big rooms with new blondwood beds (160kr per person without breakfast; doubles 400kr, 10 percent off for hostel members, Väike-Karja

1, tel. 2/443-465). The adjacent Erootika Bar looks like it's affiliated with the hostel, but it's not.

Private Rooms

Tallinn has three separate agencies which will find you a room with a local family. They're all fine and you should just go to the one that's most convenient to wherever you arrive. Fairly few people actually live in the Old Town in Tallinn, so very few private rooms are in the old section, though many are within walking distance.

The **Family Hotel Service** rents out singles for 120–200kr and doubles for 200–335kr (breakfast not included), depending on location. Rooms in the Old Town cost the most, medium-price rooms are usually a few minutes away by tram, while the cheapest rooms are a fair bus ride from the center. You can call the office (tel./fax 2/441-187) before you get to Tallinn, or you can just show up (daily 10:00–18:00, Mere puiestee 6, around the corner from the Hotel Viru; follow the signs up the driveway by the Chinese restaurant, and go in the building across the lot to the left).

At **CDS Reisid**, singles go for 295kr and doubles for 445kr (breakfast included). If you reserve ahead, they will also pick you up at the train station, ferry port, or airport for 95kr, but it's better to take a taxi (daily 9:00–17:00 from May 15–Sept. 15; Monday–Friday 10:00–16:00 from Sept. 15–May 15, Raekoja plats 17, second floor, above the Kangur shop, tel. 2/445-262, fax 631-3666.)

Rasastra is convenient for those arriving by sea (though if you reserve in advance, they'll pick you up at the dock, train-station, or airport). This office is just up the street from the dock, on the right, as you exit the ferry terminal (daily 10:00–18:00, Sadama 11, tel./fax 2/602-091). Singles cost 150kr–235kr and doubles range from 220kr–370kr, depending on location. The optional breakfast costs 20kr extra.

Eating in Tallinn

It's easy to get a good meal for $10 in Tallinn. Dozens of restaurants have opened in the Old Town in the past few years, often in cozy medieval cellars. Estonian cuisine is a satisfying northern mixture of meat, potatoes, root vegetables, and soups, with some seafood now and then. Estonia's Saku beer has an excellent reputation. Blue-labeled Saku Originaal is the most widely drunk, but some prefer darker Saku Tume. Saku Vichy and Värska are Estonia's main bottled water brands. Most restaurants accept credit cards.

Few restaurants can match **Eesli Tall** (the "Donkey Stable") for stability and convenience—it's been the most reliable dining choice in Tallinn for over five years. Everyone goes there, and so will you—expect crowds on summer weekends. The atmosphere in the upstairs section is soothing and candlelit, and there are vegetarian options on the menu. The downstairs is half-bar, half-restaurant, dungeon-walled and whitewashed, a maze of tunnels, archways, and hidden rooms. Saku goes for 21kr (Sunday–Thursday 11:00–02:00, Friday–Saturday 11:00–04:00, Dunkri 4/6, just uphill from the Town Hall).

Vanaema Juures (which translates roughly as Chez Grandma) is a small cellar restaurant which really is decorated like your grandmother's dining room—family portraits, a grandfather clock, and grandfather's attempts at painting. Enjoy homey, candlelit meals (e.g., pork roast with sauerkraut and juniper berries). Entrees run 85kr–105kr, and dinner reservations are strongly advised (Monday–Saturday 12:00–22:00, Sunday 12:00–18:00, Rataskaevu 10, tel. 631-3929).

Toomkooli serves the best fair-priced square meal on Toompea (most entrees 50kr–120kr). The menu is heavy on meat, potatoes, mushrooms, and sausage. Consider reservations (daily 12:00–23:00, Toomkooli 13, on the west edge of Toompea, tel. 2/446-613).

The **Teater Restoran** is a typical cellar restaurant with a rabbit warren of small rooms. On a cold day, order pancakes with cream and ask to sit by the fireplace. Set menus for 70kr are the best reason to come here (Lai 31, daily 9:00–01:00).

Ai Sha Ni Ya is a real Chinese restaurant with reasonable prices, a relaxing atmosphere, and chopsticks on your table. Most of the dishes are bland because Estonians aren't used to spicy food (daily 12:00–24:00, Mere puiestee 6, up a driveway from the street in the same courtyard as the Family Hotel Service, tel. 2/441-997).

Peetri Pizza is a chain with several branches in Tallinn. The Francescana is good (34kr per large one-person pizza). The take-out-only branch by the tram stop at Pärnu maantee 22, near the Palace Hotel, is open from 11:00 to 02:00 in the morning (weather dependent), and takes phone orders at 2/666-711. The branch at Kopli 2c (enter from Vana-Kalamaja) is right by the train station, in the building on the corner across from the tram stop (daily 11:00–22:00). The branch on Lai 4 has only a few seats but is just steps from the Town Hall Square (10:00–21:00).

For a less casual sit-down pizza meal, the best place is **Pizza Americana** on Harju at the corner of Müürivahe, by the WWII ruins.

Cafés: The **Maiasmokk** café and pastry shop (founded in 1864), at Pikk 16 across from the church with the old clock, is the grande dame of Tallinn cafés, and a tasty place for breakfast if you're staying at the Barn. Just point to what you want at the pastry counter, or sit down for breakfast or coffee on the other side of the shop. Everything's very cheap (Monday–Saturday 8:00–19:00, Sunday 10:00–18:00). **Hõbekass** is a larger café where you can linger and talk. There are plenty of tables in two rooms, with decent pastries and light meals (Monday–Friday 8:00–22:00, Saturday–Sunday 10:00–22:00, Harju 7, across from the World War II ruins).

For the café with the best view, try the **Neitsitorn** (Virgin Tower), the square, many-windowed tower next to Kiek in de Kök. The service and selection are still a little Soviet, but the top two floors overlook the Lower Town and serve hors d'oeuvres, pastries, and mineral water. In summer there's sometimes live classical music on the outdoor terrace. The ground level floor serves hot mulled wine (*hõõgvein*) out of wooden casks for 18kr per half-glass (daily 11:00–22:00).

These days it can seem like all Tallinn is one large Finnish nightclub, but a couple favorite spots are **Hell Hunt**, an Irish-style pub at Pikk 39, the **Von Krahli** at Rataskaevu 10, and the **Nimeta** bar at Suur-Karja 4.

For **picnics**, just about every neighborhood in Tallinn now has a Western-style self-serve grocery store with a normal mixture of local and imported goods. The convenient **Kaubahall** is a real supermarket in the center of town (Monday–Saturday 9:00–20:30, Sunday 9:00–20:00, Aia 7, not far from the twin Viru towers). The **Lembitukaubamaja**, across the bus lot from the Hotel Viru, is a smaller store open every day until 23:00.

Near Tallinn: Tartu

The obvious day trip from Tallinn is to Tartu, Estonia's university town. Tartu's old city is built in a newer, classical style no less pleasing than Tallinn's Hanseatic center. Tartu has not managed Tallinn's commercial boom, although there is now a

Peetri Pizza and a slew of Pinguin ice-cream parlors. You can put together a picnic at the Tartu Turg (market) in the center of town, then eat it on the banks of the Emajõgi River, which runs along the east side of the Old Town. Or head to the west, above the Old Town, to the set of bluffs where Tartu's ruined cathedral (partly rebuilt into an excellent museum) and early university buildings stand. The peeling paint of the 19th-century wooden houses that ring the old city, the ravines that cut through the bluffs, and the smell of coal-fired heating make parts of Tartu resemble a Massachusetts mill town.

Buses to Tartu leave roughly half-hourly from the Tallinn bus station between 6:00 and 21:00, take 2.5 hours, and cost 55kr–65kr one-way.

If you have time for a one- or two-night trip out of Tallinn and want to see the countryside, go to one of Estonia's big islands—Saaremaa or Hiiumaa. Buses take you from Tallinn to the coast at Virtsu, and then by ferry to Kuressaare, the largest town on Saaremaa, in about five hours for 90kr. The Tallinn tourist office can give you advice on booking accommodations on the islands.

Transportation Connections—Tallinn

By Train
The Tallinn train station (Balti jaam) is a short walk from the Old Town along Nunne tänav and a short, simple ride from the Hotel Viru by trams #1 or #2. This is the smallest, cleanest, and best-organized station in the Baltics, with few lines

Trains Departing Tallinn

#	To	Leaves	Arrives	2nd Class	1st Class
IK4	Moscow (Maskva)	18:27	10:50	439kr	885kr
R120	St. Petersburg (Peterburi)	22:17	9:15	177kr	356kr
IK2	Warsaw (Varssavi)	17:45	13:12	625kr	992kr

and fairly simple procedures. It has two parts: a smaller hall, at the head of the tracks, and a larger hall, which runs along the tracks. The small hall is for suburban commuter trains.

Advance purchase windows for international trains (including trains to Russia) are upstairs on the second floor of the large hall. Tickets for trains leaving the same day are available only at windows 4–6 on the ground floor of the large hall. Also on the ground floor is currency exchange, an English-speaking *informatsioon* window (daily 6:30–22:30), window 3 for returning tickets, and window 1 for processing phoned-in reservations (tel. 2/448-087 or 2/456-632).

By Bus

Tallinn's bus station (Autobussijaam) is on Tartu maantee, too far from the center to walk comfortably. Take tram #2 or #4 east from the city center to the "Bussijaam" stop, then turn the corner to your right (see our map). Buy tickets at the station. If you have a student card, ask about discounts.

Most long-distance buses to and from Tallinn also stop at the Reisisadam ferry terminal either just before or just after the bus station. Check with the driver or the station personnel to make sure.

Tallinn to Riga: In summer 1996, buses to Riga left at 9:40, 12:30, 12:45, 15:00, 19:45, 21:30, and 23:40, arriving in Riga at 15:45, 17:40, 18:55, 21:05, 01:25, 03:20, and 05:40. Fares were 96kr–100kr. Some buses are nonstop, some aren't (for example, the 12:30 bus, which continues to Vilnius, doesn't stop between Tallinn and Riga).

Tallinn to Vilnius: Buses to Vilnius left daily at 12:30 and 21:30, arriving at 22:30 and 9:20 respectively. Tickets cost 190kr.

Tallinn to St. Petersburg: Buses left at 7:30 and 16:00, arriving at 15:20 and 23:50 St. Petersburg time (an hour ahead of Tallinn) for 122kr.

By Boat

The **Reisisadam** (main ferry port) in Tallinn is at the end of Sadama tänav, about a 20-minute walk from the town square. MRP bus #2 will take you from the port to the Hotel Viru for 5kr. Trams #1 and #2 also stop five minutes from the port at the base of Sadama tänav, and you can call for a taxi. There are four terminal buildings at the port (A, B, C, and

D). The different ferry companies' signs will help you find the right one.

In 1996 Tallink hydrofoils docked at the separate **Linna-hall** terminal, about five to ten minutes' walk west from the Reisisadam and even closer to the town square.

See the Gateways chapter for full fare and schedule details on sailings to Helsinki and Stockholm. The best way to reserve a place on a ship leaving Tallinn is to call the ferry companies on the phone during business hours (Estline tel. 631-3636, Tallink 640-9877 or 640-9808, Viking 631-8193, Eestin Linjat 631-8606, Silja 631-8331 or 2/446-331). You can also visit any travel agent in town; you can stop by the ferry companies' downtown offices (e.g., the Estline office at Aia 5); or you can come to the port, where ticket offices are open whenever ships sail.

By Air
Connections between the Airport and Downtown: Tallinn's airport is the best of the five cities in this book. MRP bus #2 runs between the airport and the center of town for 5kr. The airport is quite close in, and fair taxi drivers using the meter will charge no more than about 30kr to the center.

For booking and reconfirmation: Either go to the airport or the Lufthansa City Center office at Pärnu maantee 10 (Monday–Friday 9:00–18:00, Saturday 10:00–15:00, tel. 2/444-037 or 631-4444, fax 631-3566).

RIGA, LATVIA

Tall 19th- and 20th-century buildings give Riga a cosmopolitan feel and a vertical accent unique among the Baltic capitals. Bishop Albert of Bremen, German merchants, and the Teutonic Knights made Riga the center of Baltic Christianization, commercialization, and colonization when they founded the city in the early 1200s. Under the czars, the city was the Russian Empire's busiest commercial port. Under Soviet rule, Riga became first an important military center and later, because of its high standard of living, one of the favored places for high-ranking military officers to retire to (they were given a choice of anywhere in the U.S.S.R. except Moscow, Kiev, and St. Petersburg). The Soviets encouraged Russian immigration and the percentage of residents who were Latvian plunged from well over half to about a third today.

The result is that although all the street signs are now in Latvian only, life in Riga goes on in two languages. Lithuanian and Estonian dominate Vilnius and Tallinn despite large Russian and Polish minorities, but in Riga you'll hear Russian on the street just as much as Latvian. Latvia's major newspapers, such as the daily *Diena*, come out in dual Russian and Latvian editions. And Lutheranism notwithstanding, Riga is the most Soviet-feeling Baltic capital city. It has not visibly Westernized itself as much as Tallinn. Still, Riga is far ahead of most of the former Soviet Union on the road to economic viability, and what it has done has muscle. The Latvian lat is rock-solid, and with Riga the largest city in the Baltics some predict that it is on the verge of an economic boom that will outstrip Tallinn.

Riga's Old Town is the least medieval in the Baltics. The

big churches, the moat, the bastion, fragments of the city walls, a couple dozen houses, and the cannonballs embedded in the Powder Tower are all that survive from the Middle Ages. Much of the Old Town is in 18th-century classical style; the rest of the center, and almost all of the newer parts that immediately ring it, are fine examples of late 19th- and early 20th-century building styles, particularly the Art Nouveau (Jugendstil) that betrays Riga's connections to the German-speaking world. Emerging from the Soviet period, many of these buildings no longer have quite enough warmth and life to fill their once-elegant, high-ceilinged rooms. But they are still very nice to look at. The best way to do this is to walk along the streets near the parks (such as Elizabetes iela and Alberta iela) and around the city's main commercial artery—Brīvības iela—which starts by the Freedom Monument and runs away from the Old Town and the Daugava River.

The Latvian ethnic mix is potentially the Baltics' most explosive. Russian-speakers make up about 40 percent of Latvia's population, and a majority of Riga's. Very few of them have become Latvian citizens. Yet most Russians don't want to leave; they like life in the Baltics better than life in their supposed homeland. Although it gets more media attention, the situation in Estonia is calmer and closer to being resolved. There are fewer Russians in Estonia than in Latvia, and Estonia has done a better job of trying to integrate them into Estonian society.

It is impossible to do justice to the Baltic Russian issue in just a few paragraphs, but Anatol Lieven discusses the problem thoroughly and evenhandedly in his book *The Baltic Revolution*. As a traveler, you may sense that the issue gets blown out of proportion. You will see very little Russian-Latvian and Russian-Estonian friction. Most of the service personnel in stores in Tallinn and Riga seem to switch effortlessly and naturally from one language to the next.

Perhaps the most important point in the Russo-Baltic debate is that regardless of their citizenship, residents of the Baltics enjoy clean streets, well-stocked grocery stores, stable currencies, and a far better standard of living than those in Russia. The improvement in the Baltics is a direct result of the end of Russian and Soviet domination. And ultimately, economic health is probably a prerequisite for a generous resolution of the Baltic states' ethnic questions. Estonians and

Riga

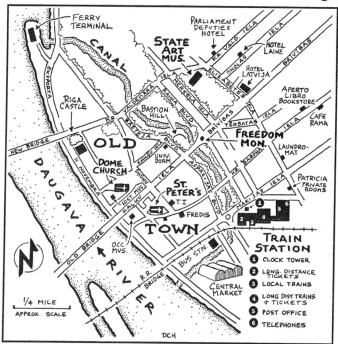

Latvians must be puzzled to see that in most of Finland, with a Swedish population of only 6 percent, all public signs and services are bilingual. Estonia and Latvia, with Russian-speaking populations of 40 and 30 percent respectively, are in full retreat from official bilingualism. The difference, of course, is that Sweden is no longer an aggressive colonizing nation, while Finns have a sense of prosperity and national security that overshadows any "threat" from the Swedes in their midst. One can only hope that the Baltics' future will be equally as calm.

Planning Your Time
Like Tallinn, Riga is worth two days but, for most, no more.

Day 1
10:00 Go up St. Peter's Church for a look around Riga.
12:00 Grab a sandwich at Fredis.

13:00   Learn your way around the Old Town, visiting the
         Dom, the Museum of the History of Riga, and the
         Occupation Museum, and buy concert tickets if there's
         anything you want to hear.
18:00   Dinner at one of the restaurants in Dome Square.

Day 2
10:00   Explore Riga's central market.
12:00   Go to the Hare Krishna café, Osiris, or Pizzeria Lulu
         for lunch.
14:00   Walk along Elizabetes iela to Alberta iela, looking at
         the Jugendstil architecture, and then visit the Art
         Museum.
16:30   Extra time for another museum or another look
         around the Old Town.
18:00   Dinner at Vērdiņš.

Orientation

Riga's Old Town is on the right bank of the Daugava, which is
very wide and crossed by only two bridges. The bus and train
stations and most sights, shops, and services are either in the
Old Town or in the 19th-century section of town immediately
around it. You should never need to venture across the river,
unless you wind up sleeping there.

Tourist Information: The tourist office (Rīgas Tūrisma
Informācijas Birojs), next to St. Peter's Church, is at Skārņu
iela 22 (daily 9:00–19:00, tel. 722-1731 or 722-2377, fax 722-
7680). It hands out free brochures and sells maps and the
handy information booklet *Riga In Your Pocket* (50 santims, also
available at kiosks or newsstands). Like its cousin *Vilnius In
Your Pocket*, it has all the indepth info on Riga that this book
doesn't have the space to cover, as well as good street and
transport maps. It's updated every two months. The erratically
available *Riga This Week* is not worth buying, but you may be
able to pick it up for free.

American Embassy: Raiņa bulvāris 7, tel. 721-0005.

Bookstore: Aperto Libro is an English-language bookstore
with a small stock including Baltic history, maps, fiction, text-
books, and dictionaries (Monday 10:00–19:00, Tuesday–Saturday
10:00–20:00, Kr. Barona iela 31, tel. 728-3810). Near-by, **Jāņa
sēta** at Elizabetes iela 83/85 is the place for maps and guidebooks
(Monday–Friday 10:00–19:00, Saturday 11:00–17:00).

Laundry: The Miele laundromat, through the archway at Elizabetes iela 85a (near Kr. Barona iela), is a savior for travelers in the Baltics. Two blocks from the train station, it has brand-new German machines and a café. Self-service costs 2.36 Ls per large load, full-service 4.12 Ls (open 24 hours, less busy on weekdays, tel. 721-7696).

Currency Exchange
0.55 lats (Ls) = about $1, 1 lat = 100 santims (s)
It's available everywhere. Rates are very competitive, so don't settle for more than a 1 percent spread between buying and selling rates. Two banks near the Dom that change American Express checks are Rīgas Komercbanka at Smilšu iela 6 and the Deutsch-Lettische Bank at Jēkaba iela 3/5.

Telephones and Mail
There is a 24-hour telephone-and-post office catty-corner from the Freedom Monument at Brīvības iela 19 (open 24 hours) and another branch at the train station. These offices and many stores will sell you the telephone cards (smallest denomination 2 Ls) that work in Riga's abundant new pay phones.

Telephone numbers in Riga come in two types: old numbers that start with 2 and new numbers that start with 7. If the phone number of the phone you're calling from starts with 7, you always dial the full seven digits of the number you're calling. If you're calling from a number that starts with 2 to another number that starts with 2, dial only the six digits following the 2; from a 2-number to a 7-number, dial 1, then the full seven digits.

2-numbers are speedily being converted to 7-numbers as the Latvian phone system goes digital, and by the time you read this, the handful of 2-numbers listed in this book may have changed. Check the latest edition of *Riga In Your Pocket*.

Getting Around Riga
Tickets for Riga's buses, trams, and trolleybuses are sold at kiosks (and by drivers) for 14s apiece. If you are staying in the center, you can walk almost everywhere. Call 070 for a taxi. Rides around the center of town should cost between 0.50 and 1.50 Ls.

Sights—Riga
▲▲▲**State Museum of Latvian Art** (Latvijas valsts mākslas muzejs)—This is the best art museum in the Baltics. The grand

staircase is impressive, but especially worthwhile is the permanent exhibition of Latvian art on the second floor. The collection, almost entirely from 1910–1940, concentrates all the
artistic and political influences that stirred Latvia then: French
impressionism, German design, and Russian propaganda-
poster style on the one hand; European internationalism, Latvian nationalism, rural romanticism, and Communism on the
other. Check out the Russian art on the first floor if you won't
make it to St. Petersburg (Wednesday–Monday 11:00–17:00,
closed Tuesday; Kr. Valdemāra iela 10).

▲▲▲**Occupation Museum** (Latvijas 50 gadu okupācijas
muzeja fonds)—A very complete exhibit covering Latvian history from 1940 to 1990, particularly the deportation of Latvians to Siberia: you can step into a replica of a gulag barracks
and see prisoners' letters home written on strips of birchbark.
Don't expect a balanced and self-critical presentation; this is a
pro-Latvian place. Full English captions. Free, but donations
accepted. (Tuesday–Saturday 11:00–17:00, closed Monday;
Strēlnieku laukums 1, near where Kaļķu iela meets the river.)

▲▲**Freedom Monument** (Brīvības piemniekelis)—Dedicated
in 1935, located on a traffic island in the middle of Brīvības
iela, this monument was strangely left standing by the Soviets.
KGB agents, however, apprehended anyone who tried to come
near it. Now it is again the symbol of independent Latvia, and
locals lay flowers between the two soldiers who stand guard at
the monument base.

▲▲**St. Peter's Church** (Pētera baznīca)—St. Peter's distinctive wooden spire, which used to be the tallest structure in
Riga, burned down during World War II. The present steel
replica was built during the Soviet period. Take the elevator up
to the observation deck for 1 lat. You can visit the inside of the
church afterwards (Tuesday–Sunday 10:00–20:00, Sept.–April
10:00–17:00, closed Monday; in the Old Town).

▲▲**Riga Dom** (Doma baznīca)—Also in the Old Town, Riga's
most formidable church dates from 1211. You can go inside for
30s (Tuesday–Friday 13:00–16:00, Saturday 10:00–14:00,
closed Monday). The inscriptions recall Latvia's German
Lutheran heritage, and in fact the crypt holds what's left of
Bishop Albert of Bremen, who started it all. The Dom has a
first-class organ and often hosts good choirs; concert tickets
(usually under 2 lats) are available at the ticket office at Riharda
Vāgnera iela 4 or downstairs in the Filharmonic building at

Amatu iela 6 (both a few blocks away and open daily 12:00–15:00 and 16:00–19:00). Just down the street from the Dom toward the river is a statue of the philosopher Johann Gottfried Herder, born in Riga in 1744, whose influential writings on nationalism were partly shaped by growing up among the Balts.

▲▲**Museum of the History of Riga and Navigation** (Rīgas vēstures un kugniecības muzejs)—Although there are only a few English labels, this large exhibit gives a fairly good idea of Riga's early history as a center on the Baltic-Black Sea trade route, explains the Old Town's street plan in terms of a now-silted-up river that used to flow through the center, and shows you everything you wanted to see on inter-war Riga. If you like the museum, you'll probably want to spend several hours exploring (50s, Wednesday–Sunday 11:00–17:00, closed Monday and Tuesday, Palasta iela 4, behind the Dom).

▲▲**Central Market** (Centrālais tirgus)—This is the most accessible and thriving central market in all of the Baltics and gives you a real insight into life here. It sprawls in and around the large former Zeppelin hangars between the train station and the river (go under the tracks).

▲▲**Other Attractions**—If you have more time, check out the **Museum of Decorative Arts** (Dekoratīvi lietikās mākslas muzejs) at Skārņu iela 10/20; the **Motor Museum** (Motormuzejs) on S. Eizenšteina iela in suburban Riga, which houses the cars of Soviet leaders, including Stalin's (take bus #21 along Brīvības iela); or even farther out, in good weather, the **Open-Air Ethnographic Museum** (Etnogrāfiskais brīvdabas muzejs), which shows farm buildings from all over Latvia (take bus #1 or #9 along Brīvības iela to the first stop across the bridge over Lake Jugla).

Near Riga: Jūrmala

A sunny summer day might be the time to go to **Jūrmala**, Riga's seaside resort. You can't swim (too polluted), but you can set up a beach chair. Go to the local-trains waiting room in the station; trains to Jūrmala are posted in red. Tickets to Majori, the most popular section of Jūrmala, are available from the windows in the same waiting room. Other popular short trips are to towns like Sigulda, Cēsis, and Valmiera along the Gauja River northeast of Riga.

Sleeping in Riga
(.55 lats = about $1)
If you're calling from the U.S., dial 011-371, then the local
number; for more phone info, see the Appendix: Direct Dialing Within the Baltics & Russia.

Hotels
The **Radi un Draugi** is an excellent small hotel right in the
Old Town with modern renovated rooms and bathrooms (singles with bath 23.60 Ls, doubles 29.50 Ls, breakfast not
included, reserve ahead; Mārstaļu iela 1, LV-1050 Riga, tel.
721-2296 or 722-0372, fax 724-2239).

   Hotel Laine is small, clean, and downtown, although
there have been persistent complaints about less-than-steam-
ing hot water. With shared bath, singles cost 12 Ls, doubles
17 Ls, and triples 24 Ls. Doubles with private baths cost
20–35 Ls. Breakfast is included. You can walk from the stations or the Old Town, or you can cross the street from the
train station and take trolleybus #3 from the stop on Merķeļa
iela for three stops; this will leave you on Kr. Valdemāra iela
around the block from the hotel. At Skolas iela 11, look for
the "Laine" sign, go into the courtyard, in the door on the far
left, and up to the reception on the third floor (tel. 728-8816,
fax 728-7658).

   The Riga **tourist information office** rents three nice
rooms with two hall bathrooms right above its office in the
Old Town. One is $30, another $40, and the third goes for
$50 (Skārņu iela 22, tel. 722-1731 or 721-2377, fax 722-7680).

   The **Parliament Members' Hotel** (Saeimas deputātu
viesnīca) indeed used to be a hotel for Supreme Soviet
deputies. It hasn't been remodeled—the bathrooms need a little work and the furniture is very old—and one has the feeling
that the members are staying elsewhere now. Still, it's in a
beautiful Art Nouveau building with a nice café, and retains
some order, civility, and shabby dignity, so it's an option if
other places are full. Sweaty backpackers will feel under-
dressed and should stay elsewhere. Walk from the station or
follow the same directions as for Hotel Laine, above. Doubles
with bath cost 24 Ls, singles 16 Ls (Kr. Valdemāra iela 23,
catty-corner from the State Museum of Latvian Art, tel. 733-
2132 or 733-4462).

   Hotel Viktorija's renovated doubles with bath are also

an option, though at 34 Ls they are more expensive than other more convenient hotels. Avoid the unrenovated rooms (A. Čaka iela 55, tel. 2/272-305, fax 2/276-209). From the train station, the hotel is 8 walkable blocks up Marijas iela (which turns into A Čaka iela); you can also hop on trolleybus #11, 18, or 23. The Alus Krogs (beer hall) Staburags on the ground floor of the Viktorija building is in the same traditional Latvian style as the Alus Sēta on Dome Square, and a good place for sauerkraut soup or a pint of Aldaris beer.

Hostelers should try to get into the **University of Latvia dormitory** at Basteja bulvāris 10 (in the Old Town about five minutes' walk from the train station, tel. 721-6221). Assorted singles and doubles with hall showers and toilets cost 2 Ls-7 Ls per room. Respectable quarters; unbeatable location; try to call ahead. It's above the Europcar office; a sign outside also says "Latvijas Universitate Studentu Kopmītnes." Fewer rooms are available in winter.

Private Rooms

Patricija Ltd. speaks English and finds rooms with families in Riga for an average of $15 per person per night without breakfast. Entire apartments (minimum three nights' stay) cost $40–$60 per night. They also do sightseeing tours and provide guides. Call ahead or stop by their office (Monday–Friday 9:00–18:00, Saturday and Sunday 9:00–13:00; very near the train station, Elizabetes iela 22, apartment 6, on the third floor up a dark stairway, tel. 728-4868, tel./fax 728-6650).

Eating in Riga

Fredis Cafe serves small, tasty, sub sandwiches in the Old Town (0.80–1.30 Ls, halves possible). Seating is limited; call ahead for large take-out orders. Vegetarian options and English menus are available (daily 9:00–24:00, Audēju iela 5, tel. 721-3731).

Vērdiņš is a French creperie and restaurant in the Old Town which has tasteful indoor and outdoor seating, and moderate prices (daily 10:00–23:00, crepes 1 Ls–2.50 Ls, entrées around 3 Ls, Mazā Pils iela 12).

Pizza Lulu bakes big whole pizzas for 5 Ls–6.50 Ls and serves slices for 69s–85s. Try the Super Lulu (daily 8:00– 24:00, Gērtrudes iela 27, near Tērbatas, for delivery call 2/361-234).

Near the Dome Square, **Alus sēta** at Tirgoņu iela 6 is a beer hall and restaurant in traditional Latvian style with self-service from the grill (daily 11:00–01:00; bean soup 80s, pork kebab 1.70 Ls, Latvian-style peas with bacon 80s). **Put Vējini** at Jauniela 18/22 has a restaurant upstairs (entrées about 3 Ls) and a bar with a fireplace downstairs (daily 11:00–24:00). In summer you can down a beer (Aldaris is Latvia's most popular brand) at the outdoor cafés in the square.

At **Rama**, cheap and filling Indian vegetarian food is dished out by, you guessed it, the International Society for Krishna Consciousness. They don't try to convert foreigners, and whatever you think of their beliefs, they do get credit for feeding a lot of hungry, impoverished Latvians and providing a place to recover from a week of fried cutlets. It's a fascinating sociological experience to see so many Eastern Europeans in face paint and saffron clothes, and where else but Riga can you eat with the Hare Krishnas without being afraid your friends will see you? (Monday–Saturday 8:00–20:30, Sunday 11:00–18:00, Kr. Barona iela 56; the café is through the front door and to the left).

Osiris, which shares an entrance with the Aperto Libro bookstore, is the kind of place to pick up a croissant and orange juice in the morning, and fine for lunch or dinner too. They have foreign newspapers on the tables and entrées for 2.50 Ls– 3 Ls (Monday–Friday 8:00–01:00, Saturday–Sunday 10:00–01:00, Kr. Barona iela 31).

Sigulda, a stand-up café at Brīvības iela and Merķeļa iela, is nothing special, but has good pastries and opens at 8:00 (Saturday–Sunday at 9:00).

For **picnic fixings**, go to the Central Market behind the train station (see Sights, above). Central Riga doesn't have a convenient modern supermarket, but most neighborhoods do have a small 24-hour grocery store.

Transportation Connections—Riga

By Train
Riga's train station (*centrālā stacija*), though not overly crowded, is confusing at first. Take a look at the Riga city map at the beginning of the chapter. The long-distance train departure hall is #4 on our map. To one side of it are ticket windows 3–10; to the other side is the entrance to the tunnel to the platforms. If you go up the stairs (rather than through the tunnel) and outside, you get more quickly to platforms 1 and 2, where most long-distance trains leave from.

Trains Departing Riga

#	To	Leaves	Arrives	2nd Class	1st Class
2	Moscow (Maskava)	17:40	11:00	20 Ls	41 Ls
4	"	18:50	12:20	20 Ls	41 Ls
38	St. Petersburg (S-Pēterburga)	19:25	8:37	17 Ls	34 Ls
221	Vilnius (Viļņa)	23:15	7:13	7 Ls	—
8	Tallinn	5:20	11:55	14 Ls	22 Ls
7	Warsaw	0:25	13:12	18 Ls	28 Ls

The local-train departure hall is #3 on our map. In its near right corner is a passage leading to hall #2 and windows 25–34.

For tickets to Moscow, St. Petersburg, and Vilnius, and other long-distance trains running on the territory of the former Soviet Union, you need to visit either windows 3–8 in hall #4 or windows 25–30 in hall #2. Your nationality doesn't matter, and it doesn't matter whether you are buying same-day or advance tickets.

For tickets on the Baltic Express to Tallinn and Warsaw, and generally on long-distance trains which are not part of the old Soviet "Express" ticketing system, you need to go to an office at Turgeņeva iela 14, 2 blocks from the train station at the corner of Timoteja iela (look for the "Dzelceļa kases" sign, Monday–Saturday 8:00–19:00, Sunday 8:00–18:00). After this office closes for the evening, windows 9–10 at the station (in hall #4) can help you with tickets on these trains.

Train #2, the *Latvijas Ekspresis* to Moscow, is Latvia's flagship. On board, conductors provide newspapers, serve meals in your compartment, and are rumored to speak English.

Trains #7 and #8 are the Estonian-run Baltic Express, which you pick up in Riga on its way between Tallinn and Warsaw (with a change of trains at Šeštokai, Lithuania). The overnight train to Tallinn has been discontinued and since taking the Baltic Express just to Tallinn is rather expensive, you should go by bus.

By Bus
The bus is the best way from Riga to Tallinn or Vilnius. Coming from the train station, Riga's bus station (*autoosta*) is on the other side of the tracks, then two minutes' walk past the central market towards the river. Buy tickets from windows 2–8 in the main hall. Watch out for the information window (#1); they charge 2 santims for questions, and 4 santims for "complicated" questions!

Try to take a bus that makes as few stops as possible en route. The buses which run from Tallinn to Vilnius via Riga (starred below) are the fastest, nonstop, and very comfortable. Be wary of the 8:10 to Vilnius, which terminates in Minsk.

Riga to Tallinn: In summer 1996 buses to Tallinn left from platform 1 at 4:10*, 6:35, 7:20, 11:50, 13:00*, 17:00, and 23:40, arriving at 9:40, 12:05, 13:20, 17:50, 18:15, 22:55, and 5:35 respectively. The fare was 4.80 Ls.

Riga to Vilnius: Buses to Vilnius left from platform 2 at 8:10, 11:00, 17:40*, 0:20, 2:00, and 3:20*, arriving five to six hours later. Tickets cost 4.20 Ls.

Riga to Warsaw: There's a daily overnight bus to Warsaw leaving at 18:00 from platform 1 (tickets 11.60 Ls).

By Boat
The ferry port in Riga is a little north of the Old Town. You can walk, but it's easier to catch a cab, or to take tram 5 or 9 to the Jūrskola stop. In 1996 the only passenger ferry service was once a week to Travemünde in Germany but there is a chance that sailings to Sweden might resume in '97. Check the latest edition of *Riga In Your Pocket*.

By Air
Connections between the Airport and Downtown: Riga's airport (*lidosta*) has been remodeled into adequate working order. If you take a taxi from (or to) the airport you will be ripped off. Instead, buy a 14s bus ticket and board bus #22, which runs between the airport and Arhitektu iela in the center of town (between the Freedom Monument and the train station).

For booking and reconfirmation: In the city, you can get tickets for most airlines at the Lufthansa City Center (Monday–Friday 9:00–18:00, Saturday 10:00–14:00, Kr. Barona iela 7/9, tel. 728-5901 or 728-5614, fax 782-8199).

VILNIUS,
LITHUANIA

Sprawling and disorganized, a Catholic church on every corner, Vilnius is the homiest and coziest of the three Baltic capitals, and also the most unsophisticated and run-down. A restful, horizontal city, Vilnius's one- and two-story buildings and its arches and courtyards are more reminiscent of a friendly Polish provincial capital than of the tall German-influenced architecture in Riga or the Hanseatic frosting-cake feel of Tallinn. No wonder, considering Lithuania's centuries-long political and religious ties with Poland, and the fact that Poland occupied Vilnius from 1920 to 1939 while most of the rest of Lithuania was independent.

Vilnius's Old Town (the buildings date largely from the 17th and 18th centuries) is huge and, unlike Riga's or Tallinn's, amazingly dilapidated: burned-out windows, crumbling wooden shutters, cracked plaster, and bowed roofs cry out for millions of dollars' worth of restoration work (while certain Soviet "improvements," like the central telephone office, cry out for the wrecking ball). The fact that Vilnius is falling apart gives the visitor a heightened sense of possibility. Every paneless window and paintless shutter makes you think of what could be there: a family, a shop, candles on the table, children playing on the floor. Riga and Tallinn, in contrast, are much more accounted for.

Vilnius's disorganization also challenges you to explore. The Old Town is full of cozy cafés and fascinating galleries and shops, but you have to duck through archways into courtyards, open gates and doors, and slowly learn your way from nook to cranny. Some streets, such as Totorių gatvė, transport you back to turn-of-the-century Eastern Europe, when Vilnius was an ethnic hodgepodge of Lithuanians, Poles, White Russians, and a booming Jewish community. These days Vilnius is half Lithuanian, half Polish and Russian, and all three languages are very much in evidence on the streets. Lithuania as a whole, however, is 80 percent Lithuanian and less than 10 percent Russian. Russian minority rights are not so big an issue here.

Paradoxically, while Lithuania is the Baltic state with the smallest Slavic population, it is the most Slavic in temperament and feel. Vilnius, as the only inland Baltic capital, was always politically and economically closer to Poland and Russia than to Scandinavia. Lithuania has a government of former Gorbachev-era reform Communists. Lithuanian politics and society have the mildly theatrical quality that you see in Russia but not in Latvia or Estonia. And Vilnius certainly feels like more of a Soviet city than Tallinn—though this is not the harsh, urban Sovietism of Riga, but rather the provincial inertia that at the same time makes Vilnius endearing.

Planning Your Time
Vilnius merits a two-day stay.

Day 1
11:00 Hike up Castle Hill and climb the tower.
13:00 Walk down Gedimino prospektas and lunch at Prie Parlamento.
14:00 Visit the Jewish Museum.
15:00 Wander through the Old Town and look into its churches, shops, and university.
18:00 Take a taxi out to dinner at Ritos smuklė.

Day 2
10:00 Visit the KGB Museum.
12:00 Lunch at Ritos Slėptuvė.
14:00 Check out the two branches of the National Museum.
18:00 End your visit with dinner at the Hotel Naujasis Vilnius.

Orientation
Vilnius' Old Town sprawls from the river and the cathedral all the way up to the train station. Walking from the station

Vilnius

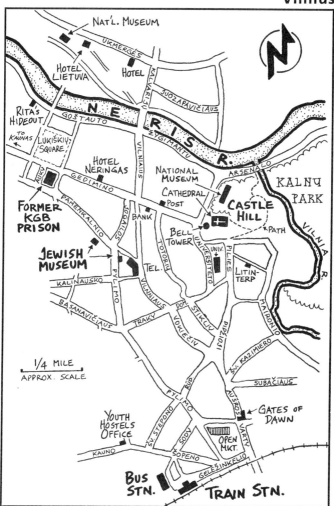

downhill to the river is pleasant. To reach the Old Town from the bus and train stations, turn right out the front door of the train station and follow Geležinkelio gatvė down the hill along the train tracks, then turn left down Aušros Vartų gatvė where the tracks cross on an overpass. Go straight through the Aušros Vartai (Gates of Dawn) and keep heading downhill.

Tourist Information: Vilnius has no tourist office. It does, however, have an incredibly good city guidebooklet called *Vilnius In Your Pocket*, written by German journalist Matthias Lüfkens, and on sale everywhere in town for 4 litas (Lt). As soon as you arrive and change money, go to the nearest kiosk and buy it for its wit, trolleybus map, and feature stories. This book can't possibly hope to better the comprehensive information in *VIYP*. We have, however, tried to save you having to mow through its masses of detail by selecting the best few restaurants, hotels, and sights. If you exhaust the restaurant or hotel choices that we've listed below, refer to *Vilnius In Your Pocket*.

American Embassy: Akmenu gatvė 6, slightly west of the Old Town, tel. 223-031 or 222-729.

Bookstore: The **Littera** bookstore in the courtyard of the university (enter from Universiteto gatvė) has maps, postcards, Penguins, and books about Lithuania in English (Monday–Thursday 10:00–18:00, Friday 10:00–17:00).

Currency Exchange
4 litas (Lt) = about $1, 1 litas = 100 centas (c)
Booths everywhere have similar rates. Among others, the Vilniaus Bankas at Gedimino prospektas 10 will exchange American Express traveler's checks for a 2 percent commission (the exchange window is open Monday–Friday 9:00–21:00, Saturday 10:00–21:00, Sunday 10:00–18:00, lunch break 12:30–13:30). The bank in the post office also exchanges traveler's checks.

Telephones and Mail
The main telephone office is on Vilniaus gatvė 33 (enter from Islandijos gatvė, open 24 hours). This is the place to buy a card (smallest denomination: 3.54 Lt) which you can use in the efficient blue Norwegian phones in this office and in phone booths around town (tear off the corner before you insert the card). Per minute, calls to Latvia or Estonia cost 1.66 Lt; to Russia, 3.54 Lt; to Europe, 5.79 Lt; and to the U.S., 10.51 Lt. There are also call-now-pay-afterwards booths in the phone office. Local calls are still free from the old-style *taksofonas* telephone booths around town.

The main post office is at Gedimino prospektas 7 (Monday–Friday 8:00–20:00, Saturday 11:00–17:00).

Getting Around Vilnius

Vilnius has trolleybuses (with overhead wires) and regular buses (without wires). Both trolleybuses and buses use named stops, and people in Vilnius often refer to their location by the name of the nearest bus stop. The trolleybuses are more convenient, because *Vilnius In Your Pocket* includes a handy map listing routes and stop names. Tickets, available from kiosks, cost 40c apiece. The crowding in Vilnius' public transportation is the worst of any of the cities covered in this book. Bus travel gets very slow—at every stop, passengers one by one unstick themselves from their neighbors to let out people even deeper inside. For the most part, we recommend riding public transportation in Vilnius only if you are with someone you feel comfortable kissing.

Taxis around the center should cost about 6–10 Lt, 10–15 Lt out to the suburbs. To summon an honest cabbie, avoid the private taxi companies and call the efficient central city-run dispatcher at 228-888 (try to find someone who speaks Lithuanian or Russian to help).

Sights—Vilnius

▲▲▲**KGB Prison**—After the KGB withdrew from Vilnius, their former prisoners set up a museum in the building where they were once held and beaten, and started giving tours to anyone who would listen. Many Lithuanians were interned here briefly before being deported to Siberia during the 1940s, and the part of the building you will see—including the cells, the padded isolation/torture chamber, appalling photographs of brutally murdered people, and piles of shredded KGB documents—is formally known as the Museum of Genocide of the People of Lithuania. Ask them to dig up their English translation of the exhibits. The museum is free, but despite these people's years of suffering they have very little budget. Consider dropping a 5-Lt coin in the donation box (Monday–Friday 10:00–16:00 though hours may vary, Gedimino prospektas 40, entrance off Aukų gatvė, tel. 622-449).

▲▲**Jewish State Museum**—Its two buildings are a block apart. The **Holocaust Exhibition** is at Pamėnkalnio gatvė 12, in the green house on the hill. Before World War II, 240,000 Jews lived in Lithuania; 95 percent of them perished during the war. Vilnius, which was 30 percent Jewish in 1914, was for many years the intellectual and cultural center of Eastern European Jewry. The exhibit first documents pre-war Jewish life in Vilnius (including blowups of powerful documentary photographs by Roman Vishniac), then its extermination by the Nazis, including one German commandant's chilling daily execution record. Admission is free, but donations are gratefully accepted. The staff will be happy to interpret if they're not busy and can also provide guided tours to Jewish historical sites around Lithuania if you contact them in advance at tel. 620-730 (Monday–Thursday 9:00–17:00, Friday 9:00–16:00, closed weekends).

The newly reopened **Exhibition on Jewish Life** is in two rooms on the second floor of Pylimo gatvė 4. One room shows relics of the city's Great Synagogue, bombed toward the end of World War II and torn down shortly thereafter. The other room is reserved for changing displays. Booklets, postcards, and crafts are on sale (Monday–Friday 11:00–17:00; free, donations accepted).

Ask the staff at either museum how to get to Paneriai, outside Vilnius, where the Nazis murdered 100,000 people, 70,000 of them Jews.

▲▲**Castle Hill**—Hike up to the top from the square near the cathedral. If it's a nice day, bring a picnic lunch. Buy a ticket (1 Lt, free on Wednesday) and climb up to the roof of **Gedimino Tower**, at the top of the hill, to see Vilnius spread out before you (and in the distance, to the west, the TV tower where Soviet troops killed 14 unarmed Lithuanians in January 1991). Gedimino Tower (Wednesday–Sunday 11:00–18:00, closed Monday and Tuesday) also houses a small museum.

▲**Lithuanian National Museum** (Lietuvos Nacionalinis Muziejus)—The second-floor exhibition on inter-war independent Lithuania is the most colorful and thus probably the most interesting to non-Lithuanian speakers (4 Lt, students 2 Lt, Wednesday–Sunday 11:00–18:00, October–April 11:00–17:00, closed Monday and Tuesday, Arsenalo gatvė 1, in the long, low building at the northwest base of Castle Hill).

The National Museum's exhibit on Lithuania from 1940 to 1991 is housed separately in a large, white, Soviet-modern building along the north riverbank (past the multi-story Hotel Lietuva). Though it's entirely in Lithuanian and Russian, the displays on the deportation and the independence struggle are very moving. Check out the tree trunk where Lithuanians nailed their discarded Soviet medals and pins in 1991 (4 Lt, students 2 Lt, Wednesdays free, Tuesday–Sunday 12:00–18:00, October–April 12:00–17:00, closed Monday).

▲**Churches**—Consider visiting the **Vilnius Cathedral** (Vilniaus Katedra), whose walls and pillars are hung with dozens of religious paintings (you might see a wedding too); **St. John's Church** (Šv. Jono) at Pilies gatvė and Šv. Jono gatvė; and the **Gates of Dawn** (Aušros Vartai) on Aušros Vartų gatvė (be sure to walk up the long hallway and the stairs to the chapel in the archway over the street).

▲**Trakai**—This picture-perfect castle is a half-hour from Vilnius, on an island in the middle of a lake. Buses leave frequently from the Vilnius bus station.

Sleeping in Vilnius

(4 Lt = about $1. If you're calling from the U.S., dial 011-370-2, then the local number; for more phone info, see the Appendix: Direct Dialing Within the Baltics & Russia.)

Hotels

The going rate for a double with bath within walking distance of the Old Town is around 250-300 Lt ($60–$75). Prepare for a functional but dated bathroom with Soviet-era tiling and plumbing, or spend a little bit more money for complete modern Western comforts.

Hotel Naujasis Vilnius is a big hotel just across the river from the Old Town with an excellent restaurant, comfortable remodeled rooms, and quite acceptable unremodeled rooms. Unremodeled singles with private bath, TV, and telephone cost 175 Lt–200 Lt, doubles 220 Lt–240 Lt; remodeled singles are 285 Lt, doubles 330 Lt. Breakfast included (Ukmergės gatvė 14; Visa, MasterCard, and Amex accepted; tel. 721-342, fax 726-750).

Hotel Pilaitė is a very small hotel near the Naujasis Vilnius, in the building with the tower on the right just across the bridge from the Old Town. The reception is on the second floor. It's central and friendly though the rooms are nothing special (singles with bath 240 Lt, doubles 280 Lt, suites 320 Lt, Kalvarijų gatvė 1, tel. 752-292, fax 752-269).

Hotel Victoria is an attractively priced Swedish-managed hotel. It has double rooms with bath for only 240 Lt—unfortunately it's not within walking distance of the main tourist sites, but you may be able to manage if you have a car or like taking buses and taxis (Saltoniškių gatvė 56, tel. 724-013, fax 724-320).

Hotel Neringas is an acceptable, clean, fairly modern hotel with a comfortable carpeted lobby. It's central but feels a little overpriced. Singles with bath 240 Lt, doubles 300 Lt, surcharge for credit card payments, breakfast included. Reception on the second floor. Reserve ahead (Gedimino prospektas 23, tel. 610-516, fax 614-160).

Zaliasis Tiltas (Green Bridge) is an old, run-down but tolerable, and very central Soviet-era hotel with a depressing lobby and a staff that is friendly but doesn't speak much English. It's not a first choice, but perhaps a fallback. Singles with bath are 150 Lt–250 Lt, doubles are 280 Lt–320 Lt (Gedimino prospektas 12, credit cards accepted, tel. 615-450 or 221-716).

Bed and Breakfasts
Litinterp can house you with a family in the Old Town for 60 Lt single or 100 Lt double, breakfast included (Monday–Friday 9:00–18:00, Saturday 9:00–16:00, Sunday closed, Bernardinų gatvė 7/2, tel. 223-291 or 223-850, fax 223-559, E-mail litinterp@omnitel.net). Also ask them about airport pickup (50 Lt), translators (350 Lt per 10-hour day), long-term apartment rentals, and car rental (260 Lt/day with unlimited mileage for a Renault 21, credit cards accepted).

Hostels
Lithuanian Youth Hostels (Lietuvos Jaunimo Nakvynės Namai) has a hostel at Filaretų gatvė 17 (tel. 696-627, fax 220-149), which you can reach directly by taking bus #34 from outside the train station and to the right to the seventh ("Filaretų") stop. The hostel has 80 beds in two- to six-bed rooms and charges 28 Lt per person.

During business hours you can stop by their main office within easy walking distance of the train station. Head left out of the train station and down Šopeno gatvė, which turns into Kauno gatvė (Monday–Friday 8:00–18:30; Kauno gatvė 1a, room 407; tel. 262-660, fax 260-631).

Eating in Vilnius
Lithuania is large enough to have a few truly distinctive culinary concoctions. If you get the chance, try *cepeliniai* (literally "zeppelins"—monstrous potato dumplings filled with meat) or *šakotis* (a two-foot-high, spiky cylindrical cake sometimes sold by the layer at cafés).

Ritos Slėptuvė (Rita's Hideout) is along the south bank of the river not far from the KGB prison museum. Chicago meets Vilnius. This dark basement hangout is run by Rita Dapkutė, a Lithuanian-American who was the director of the Lithuanian Parliament's Information Bureau during the independence struggle. The menu features spaghetti for 6 Lt–8 Lt and large pizzas for 30 Lt–50 Lt. Great burgers, too, but avoid the vegetables with rice (Monday–Thursday 7:30–02:00, Friday–Saturday 7:30–04:00, Goštauto gatvė 8). You can also order pizza delivery from Rita's at tel. 620-589.

At the **Hotel Naujasis Vilnius**, against all odds, a ground-floor dining room in a vast concrete Soviet-style hotel has been transformed into a warm and friendly place to have dinner. Those who've stayed in similar but unreformed provincial hotels in Russia may weep at the sight of this place. The menu is posted at the door, the waiters speak English and smile, there is rarely anything louder than soft piano music, candles shine on every table in the winter, and artfully prepared entrées from a wide-ranging menu average 25 Lt (daily 8:00–22:45, Ukmergės gatvė 14, in the hotel; Visa and Amex accepted).

Ritos Smuklė (Rita's Tavern) is as Lithuanian as Ritos Slėptuvė is American. This is the place to get all those Lithuanian specialities you've been hearing about in a dining room mocked up to look like a country kitchen. Two huge meat *cepeliniai* will cost you 7 Lt, and you can also get tongue, beet borscht, cabbage soup, and *blyniai* (pancakes). You'll have to take a cab (about 10–12 Lt from the Old Town, Žirmūnų gatvė 68, in the Iki supermarket complex; do your grocery shopping afterwards).

Prie Parlamento is indeed right by Parliament but not as fancy as its name suggests—it serves three meals a day at low prices from a big English-language menu. This is the place to linger over a big breakfast with friends and a newspaper (Gedimino prospektas 46, Monday–Friday 8:00–23:00, Saturday–Sunday 10:00–23:00).

Prie Universiteto, a comfy bar/restaurant in the Old Town, is a good place for late-night food (Dominikonų gatvė 9, daily 8:00–02:00).

Trys Draugai at Pilies gatvė 25a serves steaks and Hungarian food right near where all the amber and souvenir sellers congregate. It's a little expensive for Vilnius but very popular with tourists (daily 12:00–24:00).

Vilnius now has a fleet of Western-style **supermarkets** including five outlets of the home-grown **Iki** chain. The only Iki within any sort of walking distance of downtown is near Parliament at Jasinskio gatvė 16 (Jasinskio is the continuation of Pamėnkalnio and number 16 is on your left just before crossing the river, Monday–Saturday 9:00–21:00, Sunday 9:00–18:00).

Transportation Connections—Vilnius

By Train
All long-haul ticket sales are now in the large hall to the right as you enter the train station (Geležinkelio stotis). Windows 5–7 sell tickets to destinations in the former Soviet Union (daily 8:00–19:30). Windows 1–4 sell international tickets (e.g., to Poland, but you don't want to go to Poland by train). The windows straight ahead as you enter the station (#s 8–14) are only for domestic tickets.

Trains Departing Vilnius

#	To	Leaves	Arrives	2nd Class	1st Class
6	Moscow (Maskva)	16:17	9:27	131 Lt	269 Lt
26	St. Petersburg (Sankt Peterburgas)	21:32	11:30	104 Lt	209 Lt
221	Riga (Ryga)	23:20	7:15	49 Lt	—

By Bus
The Vilnius bus station is across the street from the train station. Look for the *Autobusų stotis* sign. The ticket windows are in the right half of the building. Windows 13–15, around the corner as you enter, sell tickets to all destinations outside Lithuania. There's no problem getting seats on buses although it is sensible to come a few hours in advance in case there are last-minute lines.

Vilnius to Tallinn: Buses leave daily at 8:00 and 21:45, arriving at 18:15 and 9:40; tickets cost 61 Lt.

Vilnius to Riga: Departures are at 8:00, 12:40, 17:10, 19:30, 21:45, and 0:30, arriving five to six hours later for 27 Lt–30 Lt.

Vilnius to Warsaw: Buses leave at 10:00, 19:30, 20:30, and 21:30 daily, arriving in Warsaw about ten hours later for 55 Lt–65 Lt. The 10:00 bus runs to Warszawa Zachodnia station, the 19:30 to Warszawa Wschodnia, and the 20:30 and 21:30 buses stop at both stations.

By Air

Instead of tearing down the old Stalin-era terminal at Vilnius's airport, or building a new one on a different side of the runway, they piggybacked a new terminal on top of the old one. It's a unique creation.

Connections between the Airport and Downtown: Reach the airport on bus #2 (not trolleybus #2), direction: "Aerouostas." It stops on the same side of Ukmergės gatvė as the Hotel Lietuva, then several times in the Old Town. All you need is a regular 40c bus ticket. Taxis from the airport will try to rip you off.

For booking and reconfirmation: You can buy tickets at the airport; at the Lufthansa City Center on Gedimino prospektas 37 (Monday–Friday 9:00–18:00, Saturday 9:00–14:00, tel. 223-147), or at Baltic Travel Service in the Old Town (Subačiaus gatvė 2, tel. 220 220).

Near Vilnius: Kaunas

Kaunas was Lithuania's capital between the wars when Vilnius was occupied by Poland. It's cozier, and especially friendlier to people on foot, than Vilnius. Since its population is 80 percent ethnic Lithuanian as opposed to Vilnius' 50 percent, some claim that Kaunas is the "real Lithuania."

Kaunas is an easy day trip from Vilnius. Minibuses (*mikroautobusai*) to Kaunas leave roughly on the hour from the Vilnius bus station (platform 37). The trip takes about 90 minutes. Regular-size buses run to Kaunas every half-hour and are cheaper, but take two hours. The train also takes about two hours. The Kaunas bus and train stations are only a block away from each other but more than a mile from the Old Town.

When you arrive in Kaunas, buy a copy of *Kaunas In Your Pocket* (if you didn't get one at the bus station in Vilnius), then hop into a taxi and ask to be taken to the Rotušės aikštė (**Town Hall square**). This should cost about 5 Lt–7 Lt and leave you at the central square of Kaunas's Old Town.

Kaunas

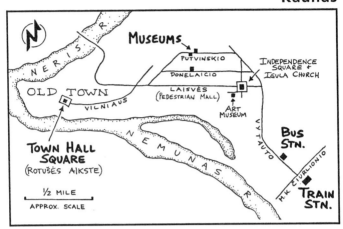

From here, you can first explore the Old Town and then walk the approximately 2 kilometers back to the station along Kaunas' grand pedestrian street, called first Vilniaus gatvė and then Laisvės aleja. There are plenty of small cafés along these streets.

One block to the left (north) of Laisvės aleja is Donelaičio gatvė, where you'll find the drab **Military Museum** of Vytautas the Great (Vytauto Didziojo Karo Muziejus), which preserves the airplane in which two Lithuanian-American aviators crashed while trying to make a nonstop New York–Kaunas flight in 1933. Behind this is the **Art Museum** (Dailės Muziejus) in whose newer wing you can listen to music by the Lithuanian composer M. K. Čiurlionis (1875–1911) and then look at paintings in which he tried to present the same structures visually. (Vytautas Landsbergis, the former Lithuanian president, first made his reputation as a Čiurlionis scholar.) The **Devil's Museum** (Velnių Muziejus), across the street at Putvinskio gatvė 64, is a collection of hundreds of folk-art devil carvings; the well-known one of Hitler and Stalin divvying up Lithuania is on the second floor. All these museums are open Wednesday through Sunday only.

If you have more time you can see the **Ninth Fort** (a notorious Nazi internment camp) or the beautiful **Pazaislis monastery** a little outside Kaunas.

Sleeping in Kaunas
(4 Lt = about $1)
If you're calling from the U.S., dial 011-370-7 before the local number; from elsewhere in Lithuania, dial 8-27 first; from elsewhere in the former Soviet Union, dial 8-0127 first.

The **Hotel Lietuva** at Daukanto gatvė 21 dates from the Soviet era but it is adequately central, clean, and reasonably priced: singles with bath cost 160 Lt, doubles with bath 240 Lt–270 Lt, breakfast included, credit cards accepted (tel. 205-992). If you're willing to pay $100 for a double room there are several nice small hotels in the Old Town now; check *Kaunas In Your Pocket* for more details. **Lithuanian Youth Hostels** puts people up at Prancūzų gatvė 59, not far from the stations, in triple rooms at $10 per room (tel. 748-972, fax 202-761).

TAKING THE TRANS-SIBERIAN RAILWAY EASTWARD

Until recently the Intourist monopoly on eastbound Trans-Siberian tickets meant that travelers in the know took the Trans-Siberian westbound, from Beijing to Moscow. Now the situation has changed, and it is arguably cheaper and easier to get tickets from Moscow to Beijing. We've met many travelers in Moscow who are on their way to Asia by rail.

There are two trains per week to Beijing: a Russian train and a Chinese train. The Russian #20 train leaves Moscow on Friday evening at 20:15, and arrives at 6:32 the following Friday morning in Beijing, a journey of a little over six days. The Chinese #4 train leaves Moscow on Tuesday evenings at 19:53 and arrives in Beijing at 15:33 the following Monday afternoon, a journey of just over 5.5 days. During the summer there is sometimes an extra Russian departure on Saturday evenings. The train station for all departures to China is Yaroslavskii Vokzal (Ярославский Вокзал) at Metro: Komsomolskaya/Комсомольская. It's the white Art Nouveau station to the right of the Metro building, and the long-distance platforms are on the far side. Arrive at the station an hour before departure.

Routes
Chinese #4 trains from Moscow and Beijing turn south through Mongolia just after they pass Lake Baikal. This route is known as the Trans-Mongolian. Russian #20 trains go around Mongolia to the east, crossing the Russian-Chinese border at Zabaikalsk/Manzhouli and passing through the Chinese city of Harbin. This route is called the Trans-Manchurian. The only train that truly measures up to the name "Trans-Siberian" is the nine-day trip between Moscow and Vladivostok in Russia's Far East.

Visas
You will need a Chinese visa, and if you take the Trans-Mongolian, a Mongolian transit visa as well. Most Chinese consulates issue tourist visas with a minimum of hassle. An exception is the consular office in Moscow (Monday, Wednesday,

Friday 9:00–12:00, ul. Druzhby/Дружбы 6, Metro:
Universitet/Университет, tel. 143-1543). They will issue
tourist visas only if you show them your ticket to China and your
onward ticket from China, or failing that, a "letter of introduction" from your country's embassy. It is better to get your Chinese visa in another country.

Moscow is, however, an excellent place to get your Mongolian transit visa. The Mongolian consular office is at Spa-
sopesovskii/Спасопесовский per. 7/1 (tel. 244-7867), just steps
from the Smolenskaya/Смоленская stop on the dark blue Metro
line. From the Metro exit, go straight through the passage under
the modern building, turn right (east) down a small street, and
walk 1 block to a park with a church on the south side and the
American ambassador's residence on the east side. The Mongolian complex is on the northwest—look for the pictures of the
camels. The consular entrance is through a marked door near
the corner of the building (Monday–Friday, 9:00–13:00). Make
sure you already have your Chinese visa to show them, and bring
your train ticket too if you have it. You should be able to pick up
your completed visa that afternoon or the next day for about $30.
Tourist (as opposed to transit) visas to Mongolia, like those to
Russia, still require an official invitation.

The Chinese Train vs. the Russian Train

Travelers on the Chinese train require a $30 Mongolian transit
visa, but this is easy to get in Moscow. The Russian train takes
about half a day longer than the Chinese train, which can be seen
as either an advantage or a disadvantage. The scenery on the two
routes is comparable.

The main difference between the two trains is inside the
cars. We highly recommend spending the extra money to go first
class. Traveling in the Chinese train's first-class, two-person
compartments can be a real pleasure: each compartment has a
table, an armchair, and a washroom (including a shower head
and occasionally lukewarm water) shared with the adjoining
compartment. The Russian train's first-class, two-person compartments are nice too, though plainer. In second class there is
less difference: in either case you're in a four-berth compartment
of the sort that is great going overnight to St. Petersburg or
Tallinn, gets awfully cramped after five days, but can be a lot of
fun if you have good company. The Chinese train also has some
first-class four-berth compartments, which should be your last

Trans-Siberian Timetable:
Moscow to Beijing

The Chinese Train

Day	Time	Station
Tues	19:53	Moscow
Wed	17:35	Perm
Thur	20:09	Novosibirsk
Fri	9:16	Krasnoyarsk
Sat	3:34	Irkutsk
	16:32	Russian-Mongolian border (arr.)
Sun	1:20	Russian-Mongolian border (dep.)
	9:00	Ulaanbaatar
	21:25	Mongolian-Chinese border (arr.)
Mon	1:51	Mongolian-Chinese border (dep.)
	15:33	Beijing

The Russian Train

Day	Time	Station
Fri	20:15	Moscow
Sat	19:16	Perm
Sun	22:11	Novosibirsk
Mon	10:50	Krasnoyarsk
Tue	5:16	Irkutsk
Wed	10:15	Russian-Chinese border (arr.)
	23:13	Russian-Chinese border (dep.)
Thur	12:09	Harbin
Fri	6:32	Beijing

Confirm schedule at station. Note that not all times are local times. For example, the Chinese train arrives in Irkutsk at 7:34 local time, since Irkutsk is 4 hours ahead of Moscow.

choice as they combine the high price of first class with the claustrophobia of having three companions.

The Chinese train has Chinese conductors and furnishings, so you may feel as if you've stepped into China already at the Moscow railway station. During the last two days of a trip on the Russian train, you may feel like you're stuck in a little capsule of Russianness that is persisting into China. This is not true in the restaurant car, which changes at each border.

Food

The food in the restaurant car is usually edible, but one such dining experience per day is enough. Before you go, visit one or more of the most well-stocked supermarkets in Moscow and load up with enough to feed yourself breakfast plus one meal a day. Some suggestions: bottled water, juice, bread and fruit for the first few days, crisp bread, peanut butter, jelly, tuna fish, chocolate, and yogurt (the kind that needs no refrigeration). Also bring instant soup, tea, and anything else that you just add hot water to, as a samovar in each car is kept boiling most of the time.

Books

Pick up either Bryn Thomas's *Trans-Siberian Handbook* or Robert Strauss's *Trans-Siberian Rail Guide*. Bring a shorter novel than *War and Peace*—on the trip you'll probably be too busy meeting your fellow travelers and buying berries from grandmothers at whistle-stop stations in Siberia to read anything really heavy.

Buying Tickets for the Trans-Siberian

From Moscow's Central Railway Agency

If you have friends in Moscow or enough time there yourself, this is the cheapest way to do it. Take the Metro to Komsomolskaya/Комсомольская, go out to the street, find Yaroslavskii Vokzal (the white, Art Nouveau station), and then look for the nine-floor, brown apartment building next to it at Krasnoprudnaya/Краснопрудная ul. 1. On the first floor of this building, on the side facing the station, is the branch of the Central Railway Agency where most people buy their Trans-Siberian tickets. You can recognize it by the sign saying Центральное Железнодорожное Агенство in green letters over the door. Head to any of windows 4–7. Prepare a piece of paper listing the number of people traveling, your name, nationality, passport number, destination, desired departure date, and desired class. The women at the ticket counters usually speak Russian only, but will probably understand your request even if it's written in Latin letters.

You don't have to come to the office in person to buy tickets. Someone else can do it for you if they come prepared with the cash and your full name, nationality, and passport number, all of which will be listed on your ticket.

Prices in 1996 were as follows: On the Russian train, approximately $175 in a second-class, four-berth compartment and $275 in a first-class, two-berth compartment; on the Chinese train, approximately $190 and $355 respectively. This represented a price *decrease* since 1995, and it would not be surprising to see fares rise again.

Demand varies considerably. Tickets to China go on sale at this office 30 days in advance. For most of the year there are no lines at the office, seats are available even just a day in advance, and you'll have your tickets in a matter of minutes. Occasionally though, during summer or during school vacations from mid-January to mid-February, bookings are heavy, lines at the office are not long but move very slowly, and you need to come two or three weeks in advance to get seats, or at least the seats you want. The Chinese trains tend to have more space than the Russian trains, because getting a Mongolian transit visa is a disincentive to many people.

From the Travellers Guest House/IRO Travel in Moscow

This is the next best alternative. In 1996 they charged $217 per person in second class and $322 per person in first class on the Russian train; $257 and $390 on the Chinese train. They may also be able to sell you tickets which allow you to stop in Irkutsk and/or Mongolia along the way. Contact them in Moscow at tel. 974-1781 or 974-1798, fax 280-7686, E-mail iro@glas.apc.org.

Other Options

The St. Petersburg International Hostel's American office at 409 N. Pacific Coast Highway, Bldg. #106, Suite 390, Redondo Beach, CA 90277 takes Trans-Siberian bookings, which they usually fill through the Travellers Guest House/IRO Travel. For specifics, contact them at tel. 310/379-4316, fax 379-8420. Any travel agency specializing in Russian travel, or any Intourist office abroad, may be able to book Trans-Siberian tickets. If you're in Finland, the international department at the Helsinki train station can write you a Trans-Siberian ticket on the spot, though there are some drawbacks (Russian train only, reconfirmation in Moscow, high markup).

APPENDIX

Baltic Timeline

1200–1300: German merchants and clerics attempt respectively to colonize the Baltic states and Christianize their native populations. A German class of land-owning nobles emerges in Estonia and Latvia. Lithuania resists.

1386: Preferring the Poles to the Germans, the Prince of Lithuania marries the Princess of Poland and unites the two countries. Catholicism becomes the state religion.

1520s: The Reformation reaches Estonia and Latvia.

1629: Sweden acquires most of Estonia and Latvia.

1700–1721: Russia wins Estonia and Latvia from Sweden in the Great Northern War.

1795: Lithuania becomes part of the Russian Empire in the third partition of Poland.

1850–1890: Independence movements start to roll. Ethnic and national consciousness grows in the Baltics.

1918–1921: The Baltics gain independence in the wake of the Russian Revolution and the First World War, but have to fight both the Germans and the Red Army for it. Ethnic Germans start leaving Estonia and Latvia.

1939: The secret Molotov-Ribbentrop pact between Hitler's Germany and Stalin's Russia declares the Baltic states part of Russia's sphere of influence.

1940–1945: The Baltics become a political football between Russia and Germany. Net result: Mass deportations of Balts to Siberia and of Jews to the Nazi concentration camps, and the Soviet annexation of all three Baltic states.

1945–1989:   Sovietization. Ethnic Russians move into the
                 Baltics to take military and civilian jobs.

1989–1991:   Under *glasnost*, a mass movement for an end to
                 Soviet occupation and the restoration of inde-
                 pendence gains steam. Lithuania declares
                 independence first; Moscow's armed reprisals
                 leave 14 dead in Vilnius.

August 1991: World recognition of Baltic independence
                 comes in the wake of the failed coup in
                 Moscow.

Russian Timeline

800s: Spurred by Viking trade along Russia's rivers,
                 states form around the cities of Novgorod and
                 Kiev. ("Russia" comes from a Viking word.)

988:   Kiev converts to Christianity and becomes part
                 of the Eastern Orthodox world.

1224–1242:   The Mongol hordes invade Russia, conquer,
                 and exact tribute. Russia, however, succeeds
                 where the Baltics failed: at keeping the Ger-
                 mans out.

1465–1557:   The Russian czars consolidate power in
                 Moscow, drive away the Mongols, and form a
                 unified Russian state.

1613:   Foundation of the Romanov dynasty, which
                 lasts until 1917.

1703:   Czar Peter the Great founds St. Petersburg as
                 Russia's "window on the West." Major phase
                 of southward and eastward Russian expansion
                 under Peter and his successor Catherine.

1812:   Napoleon burns Moscow, but loses an army
                 on the way home.

1855–1861:   Russia loses Crimean War and decides to
                 modernize, including freeing the serfs.

1905:   Russia loses a war with the Japanese,

contributing to a failed revolution later glorified by the Communists as a manifestation of worker's consciousness.

1917: In March, the czar is ousted by a Provisional Government led by Aleksandr Kerensky.

1917: In November, the Provisional Government is ousted by the Bolsheviks (Communists), led by Lenin.

1924–1939: Stalin purges the government and the army, and forced collectivization causes famine and tens of millions of deaths in Ukraine.

1939–1945: World War II. Russia loses another 20 million to the Germans, but winds up with control over a sizable chunk of Eastern Europe.

1945–1962: Peak of the Cold War. Russia acquires the atom bomb and launches the first satellite and the first manned space mission.

1970s: The "time of stagnation" under Leonid Brezhnev. The failure of the Communist economy becomes more and more apparent.

1985: Mikhail Gorbachev comes to power and declares the beginning of *glasnost* (openness) and *perestroika* (restructuring).

1991: Reactionaries try to topple Gorbachev. They fail to keep power, but so does Gorbachev. Boris Yeltsin takes control of the government and starts reforms.

1993: Reactionaries try to topple Yeltsin. They fail to gain power, but Yeltsin is weakened.

1995–96: Boris Yeltsin hangs on to power despite grumbling from the ultra-nationalist right and the communist left.

1997: Stay tuned . . .

Let's Talk Telephones

In Europe, card-operated public phones are speedily replacing coin-operated phones. Each country sells telephone cards good for use in its country. Get a phone card at any post office. To make a call, pick up the receiver, insert your card in the slot in the phone, dial your number, make your call, then retrieve your card. The price of your call is automatically deducted from your card as you use it. If you have a phone card phobia, you'll usually find easy-to-use "talk now-pay later" metered phones in post offices. Avoid using hotel room phones, which are major rip-offs for anything other than local calls and calling card calls (see below).

Calling Card Calls

Calling home is easy from any type of phone if you have an AT&T calling card. From a private phone, just dial the toll-free number to reach the operator. Using a public phone, first insert a small-value coin or a Russian or Baltic phone card. Then dial the operator, who will ask you for your calling card number and place your call. Your bill awaits you at home (one more reason to prolong your vacation). For more information, see Introduction: Telephones and Mail.

AT&T's USA Direct Service

In . . .	Dial . . .
Lithuania	8-(wait for tone)-196
Latvia	700-7007
	(from 2-numbers dial 827-007-007)
Estonia	810-800-1001
Moscow	755-5042
St. Petersburg	325-5042

Dialing Direct

Calling Between Countries: First dial the international access code, then the country code, followed by the area code, then the local number. In most of Europe, you dial the area code in full if you're calling within the country, but drop the initial zero when calling from outside the country (though this does not apply to the Baltics and Russia—see Dialing Direct Within the Baltics and Russia, below).

Calling Long Distance Within a Country: First dial the area code, then the local number.

   Some of Europe's Exceptions: A few countries lack area codes, such as Denmark, Norway, and France; Latvia and Estonia are starting to follow this pattern too. You still use the above sequence and codes to dial, just skip the area code.

International Access Codes
When dialing direct, first dial the international access code of the country you're calling from.

Austria: 00	Latvia: 00
Belgium: 00	Lithuania: 810
Britain: 00	Netherlands: 09
Czech Republic: 00	Norway: 00
Denmark: 00	Portugal: 00
Estonia: 800	Russia: 810
Finland: 990	Spain: 07
France: 00	Sweden: 009
Germany: 00	Switzerland: 00
Ireland: 00	U.S.A./Canada: 011
Italy: 00	

Country Codes
After you've dialed the international access code, then dial the code of the country you're calling.

Austria: 43	Latvia: 371
Belgium: 32	Lithuania: 370
Britain: 44	Netherlands: 31
Czech Republic: 42	Norway: 47
Denmark: 45	Portugal: 351
Estonia: 372	Russia: 7
Finland: 358	Spain: 34
France: 33	Sweden: 46
Germany: 49	Switzerland: 41
Ireland: 353	U.S.A./Canada: 1
Italy: 39	

Dialing Direct Within the Baltics & Russia

This is the sequence of numbers you dial when calling direct in the Baltics and Russia. "X" stands for any local telephone number listed in this book (including the initial "2" on some Tallinn and Riga numbers). So to dial local number 2/234-567 or 654-3210 in Tallinn from the U.S.A., dial 011-372-2234567 or 011-372-6543210. Baltic phone numbering is rapidly evolving, so remember that this chart is based on a June 1996 snapshot of the system.

Dialing Direct Codes

	To Moscow	St. Pete	Tallinn	Riga	Vilnius	U.S.A.
From						
Moscow	—	8-812-x	8-014-x	8-013-x	8-012-2-x	8-10-1-x
St. Pete	8-095-x	—	8-014-x	8-013-x	8-012-2-x	8-10-1-x
Tallinn	800-7-095-x	800-7-812-x	—	800-371-x	800-370-2-x	800-1-x
Riga*	00-7-095-x	00-7-812-x	00-372-x	—	00-370-2-x	00-1-x
Vilnius	8-095-x	8-812-x	8-014-x	8-013-x	—	8-10-1-x
U.S.A.	011-7-095-x	011-7-812-x	011-372-x	011-371-x	011-370-2-x	—

*From 7-numbers only. From 2-numbers, dial the same codes as from Vilnius.

Climate

Average high/low temperatures (Fahrenheit) and average rainy days per month

City	Jan	Mar	May	July	Sept	Nov
Helsinki/ Tallinn	26°/17° 20	32°/20° 14	56°/40° 12	71°/55° 14	59°/46° 15	37°/30° 19
Moscow	15°/3° 18	32°/18° 15	66°/46° 13	73°/55° 15	61°/45° 13	35°/26° 15
Riga/ Vilnius	25°/14° 19	35°/20° 16	61°/42° 13	71°/52° 12	63°/47° 17	39°/30° 19
St. Petersburg	19°/8° 21	32°/18° 14	59°/42° 13	70°/55° 13	60°/47° 17	35°/28° 18
Warsaw	32°/22° 15	42°/28° 11	67°/48° 11	75°/58° 16	66°/49° 12	42°/33° 12

Metric Conversion (approximate)

1 inch = 25 millimeters   32 degrees F = 0 degrees C
1 foot = 0.3 meter   82 degrees F = about 28 degrees C
1 yard = 0.9 meter   1 ounce = 28 grams
1 mile = 1.6 kilometers   1 kilogram = 2.2 pounds
1 centimeter = 0.4 inch   1 quart = 0.95 liter
1 meter = 39.4 inches   1 square yard = 0.8 square meter
1 kilometer = .62 mile   1 acre = 0.4 hectare

Numbers and Stumblers

•Europeans write a few of their numbers differently than we do.
1 = 1 , 4 = 4 , 7 = 7. Learn the difference or miss your train.
•In Europe, dates appear as day/month/year, so Christmas is
25-12-97.
•Commas are decimal points and decimals commas. A dollar
and a half is 1,50 and there are 5.280 feet in a mile.
•When pointing, use your whole hand, palm downward.
•When counting with fingers, start with your thumb. If you
hold up your first finger to request one item, you'll probably
get two.
•What we Americans call the second floor of a building is the
first floor in Europe.
•Europeans keep the left "lane" open for passing on escalators
and moving sidewalks. Keep to the right.

Public Holidays

Russia: Jan. 1 (New Year's), Jan. 7 (Christmas), March 8
(Women's Day), May 1, May 9 (Victory Day), June 12 (Independence Day), Dec. 31 (New Year's Eve).

Estonia: Jan. 1 (New Year's), Feb. 24 (Independence Day),
Good Friday, Easter, May 1, June 23 (Victory Day), June 24
(Midsummer), Nov. 16 (Rebirth Day), Dec. 25–26 (Christmas).

Latvia: Jan. 1 (New Year's), Good Friday, Easter, May 1, June
23–24 (Midsummer), Nov. 18 (Independence Day), Dec.
25–26 (Christmas), Dec. 31 (New Year's Eve).

Lithuania: Jan. 1 (New Year's), Feb. 16 (Independence Day),
Good Friday, Easter (Sunday and Monday), May 1, July 6
(Statehood Day), Nov. 1 (All Saints), Dec. 25–26 (Christmas).

Learning Cyrillic

The next three pages contain practical language information that you should tear out and keep in your pocket for those times when you are separated from your guidebook.

Russia uses the Cyrillic alphabet. If you spend 15 minutes learning it, you'll be able to read maps, street signs, food labels, subway directions, train schedules, menus, inscriptions, names of famous people, and Russian graffiti. Ignore Cyrillic, and you'll be completely unable to get around on public transportation, unable even to write the name of a destination for a taxi driver or train-ticket seller, unable to read a street sign, and totally reliant on English-speaking (hard-cash–hungry) Russians. Tape this rip-out cheat sheet to the inside of your glasses. Chant it before going to sleep. Do whatever you need to do—just learn it. Also, some people don't realize that you can read Cyrillic words out loud. When you say Nevsky Prospekt, you're also saying Невский Проспект.

Cyrillic	English spelling	*Sounds like:*	Cyrillic	English spelling	*Sounds like:*
А а	a	Rach*m*aninoff	Т т	t	*T*urgenev
Б б	b	*B*aryshnikov	У у	u	*U*stinov
В в	v	Uncle *V*anya	Ф ф	f	*F*runze
Г г	g	*G*ogol	Х х	kh	as in the
Д д	d	*D*ostoevskii			Scottish lo*ch*
Е е	e	*Y*eltsin	Ц ц	ts	*Ts*arevich
Ё ё	yo	*Y*ossarian	Ч ч	ch	*Tch*aikovsky
Ж ж	zh	Brez*h*nev	Ш ш	sh	Pu*sh*kin
З з	z	*Z*amiatin	Щ щ	shch	Khru*shch*ev
И и	i	*I*zvestiya	Ъ ъ	—	"hard sign"
Й й	i	Tolstoy			(ignore it)
К к	k	*C*atherine	Ы ы	y	Solzhenitsyn
Л л	l	*L*enin	Ь ь	—	"soft sign"
М м	m	*M*olotov			(ignore it)
Н н	n	*N*abokov	Э э	e	*E*thelr*e*d the
О о	o	*O*blomov			Unr*ea*dy
П п	p	*P*asternak			
Р р	r	*R*asputin	Ю ю	yu	*Yu*goslavia
С с	s	*S*uvorov	Я я	ya	*Ya*lta

Survival Phrases

In the following list, pronounce *a* as in car, *e* as in bet, *i* as in spaghetti, *o* as in more, *u* as in tune. ä, ö, and ü in Estonian have the same sounds as umlauts in German (*ä* is like the English *a* in cat; for *ö* and *ü*, try to say "e" with your lips rounded).

English	Estonian	Latvian	Lithuanian	Russian
yes	**ya**	yā	**taip**	da
no	**ei**	nē	**ne**	nyet
hello	*te*re	*lab*dien	*la*ba di*e*na	*zdra*sstvuy-tye
goodbye	**head** *ae*ga	*vi*su*gai*shu	**vi**so **gero**	do svi*da*nya
Please	*pa*lun	*lu*dzu	*pra*shom	paz*hal*sta
thank you	**tänan**	*pal*dies	*a*chu	spas*i*ba
excuse me	*va*bandage	*at*vainoyiet	atsipras*hau*	izvi*ni*tye
one	**üks**	viens	*vi*enas	a*din*
two	**kaks**	divs	**du**	dva
three	**kolm**	tris	**tris**	tri
Where is...?	**Kus on...?**	Kur ir...?	**Kur...?**	Gdye...?
How much?	**Kui** *pa*lyu *mak*sab?	Tsik *mak*sā?	**Kiek** *kai*nuoya?	*Skol*ka *stoy*it?
I don't understand	**Ma ei sa** *a*ru	Es *ne*saprotu	**Ash** *ne*su*pran*tu	Nye *p*onil
Do you speak English?	**Kas te***ie* **räägite** *ing*lise **keelt?**	*Vai* jūs runā*jet*-*an*gliski?	**Ar** *kal*bates *an*glishkai?	Vi gava*ri*-tye pa an*glis*ki?

Buying Train Tickets

Please help me to buy the following tickets:
Пожалуйста; помагите мене купить эти билеты:

Destination/До станции _____
Month/Месяц: _____ Date/Число: _____
Train number/Поезд Nr _____
Departure time/Отправление в _____

Number of passengers/Количество человек: _____
Class/Тип: 2-berth/СВ
4-berth/купейный
Sitting place/Сиденный

Surname(s)/Фамипия: _____
Citizenship/Гражданство: _____

Нет мест.
There are no seats available.

Мест ест; но в другом классе.
There are seats, but only in a different class.

Здесь не продаём.
We don't sell these tickets at this window.

Road Scholar Feedback for Baltics & Russia 1997

We're all in the same travelers' school of hard knocks. Your feedback helps us improve this guidebook for future travelers. Please fill this out (attach more info or any tips/favorite discoveries if you like) and send it to us. As thanks for your help, we'll send you our quarterly travel newsletter free for one year. Thanks! **Rick**

I traveled mainly by: ___ Car ___ Train/bus tickets
___ Railpass   Other (please list _____)

Number of people traveling together:
___ Solo ___ 2 ___ 3 ___ 4 ___ Over 4 ___ Tour

Ages of traveler/s (including children):

_____

I visited _____ countries in _____ weeks.

I traveled in: ___ Spring ___ Summer ___ Fall ___ Winter

My daily budget per person (excluding transportation):
___ Under $40 ___ $40–$60 ___ $60–$80 ___ $80–$120
___ over $120 ___ Don't know

Average cost of hotel rooms: Single room $_____
Double room $_____   Other (type _____) $_____

Favorite tip from this book:

_____

Biggest waste of time or money caused by this book:

_____

Other Rick Steves books used for this trip:

_____

Hotel listings from this book should be geared toward places that are:
___Cheaper   ___More expensive   ___About the same

Of the recommended accommodations/restaurants used, which was:

Best _____

    Why? _____

Worst _____

    Why? _____

I reserved rooms:

____from USA   ____in advance as I traveled

____same day by phone   ____just showed up

Getting rooms in recommended hotels was:

____easy   ____mixed   ____frustrating

Of the sights/experiences/destinations recommended by this book, which was:

Most overrated _____

    Why? _____

Most underrated _____

    Why? _____

Best ways to improve this book:

_____

I'd like a free newsletter subscription:

___ Yes   ___ No   ___ Already on list

_____

Name

_____

Address

_____

City, State, Zip

Please send to:
Europe Through the Back Door,
Box 2009, Edmonds, WA 98020

Faxing Your Hotel Reservation

Most hotel managers know basic "hotel English." Faxing is the preferred method for reserving a room. It's more accurate and cheaper than telephoning and much faster than writing a letter. Use this handy form for your fax. Photocopy and fax away.

One-Page Fax

To: _____ @ _____
         hotel   *fax*

From: _____ @ _____
           name   *fax*

Today's date: ___ / ___ / ___
                 day   month   year

Dear Hotel _____,

Please make this reservation for me:

Name: _____

Total # of people: _____   # of rooms: _____   # of nights: _____

Arriving: ___ / ___ / ___   My time of arrival (24-hr clock): _____
              day   month   year   (I will telephone if I will be late)

Departing: ___ / ___ / ___
               day   month   year

Room(s): Single___ Double___ Twin___ Triple___ Quad___

With: Toilet___ Shower___ Bath___ Sink only___

Special needs: View___ Quiet___ Cheapest Room___

Credit card: Visa___ MasterCard___ American Express___

Card #: _____

Expiration Date:_____

Name on card: _____

You may charge me for the first night as a deposit. Please fax or mail me confirmation of my reservation, along with the type of room reserved, the price, and whether the price includes breakfast. Thank you.

_____
Signature

_____
Name

_____
Address

_____
City   *State*   *Zip Code*   *Country*

INDEX

Accommodations, 17–18; *See also* Lodging
Airports: Moscow, 68; Riga, 118; St. Petersburg, 89; Tallinn, 92–106; Vilnius, 129

Banking, 7

Climate chart, 142
Consulates, Russian, 31–32
Cyrillic, 144–146

Dostoevski, 78

Eating, 18–20
Estonia, 92–106
Exchange rates, 4

Guidebooks, 9–10

Health, 20–21
Helsinki, 33–43
Hermitage, 74
History: Baltic, 137–138; Russian, 138–139
Holidays, 143
Hotels, 17–18; *See also* Lodging

Jūrmala, 113

Kaunas, 129–130
Kremlin, 56–57

Language, 7–8, 144–145
Latvia, 107–118
Lithuania, 119–130

Lodging and food
Kaunas, 130
Moscow, 61–65
Riga, 114–116
St. Petersburg, 80–86
Tallinn, 99–103
Vilnius, 125–128
Money, 4
Moscow, 50–68; Travellers Guest House, 28, 62, 81, 136

Philosophy, Back Door, 25
Pushkin Museum, 58

Restaurants, 19
Riga, 107–118
Russia, surviving, 21–23

Saaremaa, 103–104
Safety, 20–21
Sightseeing Priorities, 5–6
St. Petersburg, 69–89; International Hostel, 27, 62, 80–81, 135
Stockholm, 43–44

Tallinn, 92–106
Tartu, 103–104
Taxis, 14–15
Telephones, 15–17, 140–142
Trains, 11–13, 146
Transportation, 11–15; Moscow, 66–68; Riga, 116–118; St. Petersburg, 86–90; Tallinn, 104–106; Trans-Siberian, 132–136; Vilnius, 128–129
Trans-Siberian, 132–136
Travellers Guest House, 28, 62, 81, 136

Valmiera, 113
Vilnius, 119–131
Visas: Baltic, 26; Belarussian,
  47; Chinese, 132–133;
  Mongolian, 132–133; Polish,
  44–45; Russian, 26–32

Warsaw, 44–47
Water, 20
When to go, 5

Rick Steves' Phrase Books

Unlike other phrase books and dictionaries on the market, my well-tested phrases and key words cover every situation a traveler is likely to encounter. With these books you'll laugh with your cabby, disarm street thieves with insults, and charm new European friends.

Each book in the series is 4" x 6", with maps.

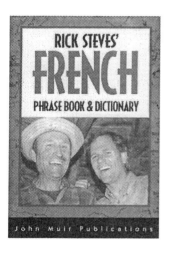
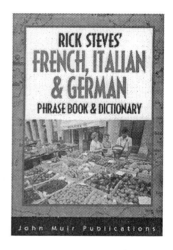

RICK STEVES' FRENCH PHRASE BOOK & DICTIONARY
U.S. $5.95/Canada $8.50

RICK STEVES' GERMAN PHRASE BOOK & DICTIONARY
U.S. $5.95/Canada $8.50

RICK STEVES' ITALIAN PHRASE BOOK & DICTIONARY
U.S. $5.95/Canada $8.50

RICK STEVES' SPANISH & PORTUGUESE PHRASE BOOK
& DICTIONARY
U.S. $7.95/Canada $11.25

RICK STEVES' FRENCH, ITALIAN & GERMAN PHRASE
BOOK & DICTIONARY
U.S. $7.95/Canada $11.25

Other Books from John Muir Publications

Rick Steves' Books

Asia Through the Back
Door, $17.95
Europe 101: History
and Art for the Trav-
eler, $17.95
Mona Winks: Self-
Guided Tours of
Europe's Top
Museums, $18.95
Rick Steves' Baltics &
Russia, $9.95
Rick Steves' Europe,
$18.95
Rick Steves' France,
Belgium & the Nether-
lands, $15.95
Rick Steves' Germany,
Austria & Switzerland,
$14.95
Rick Steves' Great
Britain & Ireland
$15.95
Rick Steves' Italy,
$13.95
Rick Steves' Scandi-
navia, $13.95
Rick Steves' Spain &
Portugal, $13.95
Rick Steves' Europe
Through the Back
Door, $19.95
Rick Steves' French
Phrase Book, $5.95
Rick Steves' German
Phrase Book, $5.95
Rick Steves' Italian
Phrase Book, $5.95
Rick Steves' Spanish &
Portugese Phrase
Book, $7.95
Rick Steves' French/
German/Italian Phrase
Book, $7.95

A Natural
Destination Series

Belize: A Natural Desti-
nation, $16.95
Costa Rica: A Natural
Destination, $18.95
Guatemala: A Natural
Destination, $16.95

City•Smart™
Guidebook Series

City•Smart Guidebook:
Cleveland, $14.95
City•Smart Guidebook:
Denver, $14.95
City•Smart Guidebook:
Minneapolis/St. Paul,
$14.95
City•Smart Guidebook:
Nashville, $14.95
City•Smart Guidebook:
Portland, $14.95
City•Smart Guidebook:
Tampa/St. Petersburg,
$14.95

Travel+Smart™
Trip Planners

American Southwest
Travel+Smart Trip
Planner, $14.95
Colorado Travel+
Smart Trip Planner,
$14.95
Eastern Canada
Travel+Smart Trip
Planner, $15.95
Florida Gulf Coast
Travel+Smart Trip
Planner, $14.95
Hawaii Travel+Smart
Trip Planner, $14.95
Kentucky/Tennessee
Travel+Smart Trip
Planner, $14.95
Minnesota/Wisconsin
Travel+Smart Trip
Planner, $14.95
New England
Travel+Smart Trip
Planner, $14.95
Northern California
Travel+Smart Trip
Planner, $15.95
Pacific Northwest
Travel+Smart Trip
Planner, $14.95

Other Terrific
Travel Titles

The 100 Best Small Art
Towns in America,
$15.95
The Big Book of
Adventure Travel,
$17.95

Indian America: A Trav-
eler's Companion,
$18.95
The People's Guide to
Mexico, $19.95
Ranch Vacations: The
Complete Guide to
Guest and Resort,
Fly-Fishing, and
Cross-Country Skiing
Ranches, $22.95
Understanding Euro-
peans, $14.95
Undiscovered Islands
of the Caribbean,
$16.95
Watch It Made in the
U.S.A.: A Visitor's
Guide to the Compa-
nies that Make Your
Favorite Products,
$16.95
The World Awaits,
$16.95
The Birder's Guide to
Bed and Breakfasts:
U.S. and Canada,
$17.95

Automotive Titles

The Greaseless Guide
to Car Care, $19.95
How to Keep Your
Subaru Alive, $21.95
How to Keep Your Toy-
ota Pickup Alive,
$21.95
How to Keep Your VW
Alive, $25

Ordering
Information

Please check your local
bookstore for our books,
or call **1-800-888-7504** to
order direct and to
receive a complete cata-
log. A shipping charge
will be added to your
order total.

Send all inquiries to:
John Muir Publications
P.O. Box 613
Santa Fe, NM 87504